Report #: I733-032R-2006
Date: December 2006

# *Oracle Application Server on Windows 2003 Security Guide*

## Enterprise Applications Division
### of the
## Systems and Network Attack Center (SNAC)

## Information Assurance Directorate

**National Security Agency**
**ATTN: I733**
**9800 Savage Road STE 6704**
**Ft. Meade, Maryland 20755-6704**
**410-854-6191 commercial**
**410-859-6510 facsimile**

## Acknowledgment

We thank the MITRE Corporation for its collaborative effort in the development of this guide. Working closely with our NSA representatives, the MITRE team—John Carlson, Yi-Fang Koh, Harvey Rubinovitz, and Jackson Wynn—generated the security recommendations in this guide.

## Warnings

This document provides security guidance for Oracle Application Server 10g Enterprise Edition installed on Windows Server 2003 platforms. The recommendations contained herein are not applicable to other versions of Oracle Application Server, other commercial J2EE application server products, or to other Windows or non-Windows platforms.

Do not attempt to implement any of the recommendations in this security guide without first testing in a non-operational environment. Application of these recommendations to systems deployed in a production environment may result in loss or corruption of stored data, and/or affect the operational status of those systems.

# Trademark Information

Microsoft® and Windows® are registered trademarks of Microsoft Corporation in the U.S.A. and other countries.

Java® is a registered trademark of Sun Microsystems.

All other names are registered trademarks or trademarks of their respective companies.

# Table of Contents

## Table of Figures

## Table of Tables

# Introduction

This document provides security guidance on the installation, configuration and use of Oracle Application Server 10g Enterprise Edition (OAS 10g EE) running on Windows Server 2003. OAS 10g EE is a J2EE-compliant application server developed by Oracle, Inc. This guide discusses security-relevant recommendations for OAS 10g EE running on Microsoft Windows Server 2003 and does not consider the installation, configuration or operation of this product on other Windows or non-Windows platforms.

This document is not intended to replace existing OAS product documentation. It is assumed that the reader is familiar with the OAS document set and will refer to product documentation as needed in order to implement recommendations contained in this guide.

It is also assumed that the reader is familiar with Windows 2003 Server administration and is able to create and manage user accounts and groups; configure access controls, account policies and user rights; modify and view registry settings; configure auditing; review audit and event logs; and other daily administration tasks.

Lastly, this document assumes that the baseline platform configuration of the Windows Server 2003 server and Oracle Application Server 10g EE are up-to-date in terms of installed security updates, patches and/or service packs.

## Organization of this Guide

This document consists of the following chapters:

**Chapter 1 - OAS Deployment Considerations** discusses security considerations and recommendations for deploying OAS 10g EE in an enterprise environment.

**Chapter 2 – OAS Installation** discusses security considerations and recommendations for installing OAS 10g EE on Windows Server 2003 hosts.

**Chapter 3 - OAS HTTP Server** discusses security considerations and recommendations for configuring the OAS HTTP Server.

**Chapter 4 - OAS Portal** discusses security considerations and recommendations for configuring the OAS Portal.

**Chapter 5 - OAS Web Cache** discusses security considerations and recommendations for the OAS Web Cache.

**Chapter 6 - OAS Identity Management** discusses security considerations and recommendations for configuring OAS Identity Management.

**Chapter 7 - Summary of Security Points** summarizes security recommendations that are discussed throughout this security guide.

## Getting the Most from this Guide

The following list contains suggestions to ensure successful use of this guide:

❑ Always perform a complete backup of a Windows Server 2003 before implementing any of the recommendations in this guide.

❑ Work from a comprehensive deployment plan that considers availability, scalability and security requirements of the operational environment into which Oracle Application Servers are being installed.

❑ Review the Oracle Application Server product documentation, particularly the concepts, installation, and administrator's guides before reading this document.

❑ Read this guide in its entirety. Omitting steps can potentially lead to an unstable system, requiring reinstallation of Oracle product software.

❑ Prior to installing Oracle Application Server, start with a Windows Server 2003 platform configured with the latest service packs and security patches, hardened as appropriate.

# OAS Deployment Considerations

## Introduction

Deployment considerations include issues that arise in the course of planning for a deployment of OAS 10g EE in an enterprise environment. In an enterprise environment, OAS 10g EE product tiers can be deployed to different server platforms. This distributed server architecture gives rise to unique security issues that must be considered as part of deployment planning and installation.

This chapter discusses deployment considerations for distributed systems in general and for OAS 10g EE in particular. General deployment considerations including use of firewalls, platform hardening, Public Key Infrastructure (PKI) and distributed system performance are discussed in the next section. The sections that follow discuss OAS 10g EE product-specific deployment considerations and recommendations, and provide a summary of important security points raised in this chapter.

## General Deployment Considerations

### Firewalls and Layered Security

The use of firewalls within the security perimeter provides layered security, which is especially important for distributed, enterprise systems such as OAS 10g EE. A firewall is a network device that controls network traffic between different zones of trust in accordance with established security policies. A firewall controls network traffic by allowing only certain protocol messages to pass.

An external firewall is deployed at the security perimeter to control network traffic between the system and external users, that is, users outside the security perimeter. The external firewall serves as a demarcation point for the De-Militarized Zone (DMZ), which is a region of the network used to separate the external network environment from the enterprise network on which host systems are deployed. Deployment of an external firewall and DMZ is considered a security best practice that is often required in order to connect to a public Internet.

Firewalls can also be deployed within the security perimeter to control network traffic generated internally. Internal firewalls establish protection zones within the security perimeter and can provide some mitigation of risks associated with insider threats.

The following illustration depicts one possible deployment strategy to partition OAS 10g EE application components into different protection zones using firewalls.

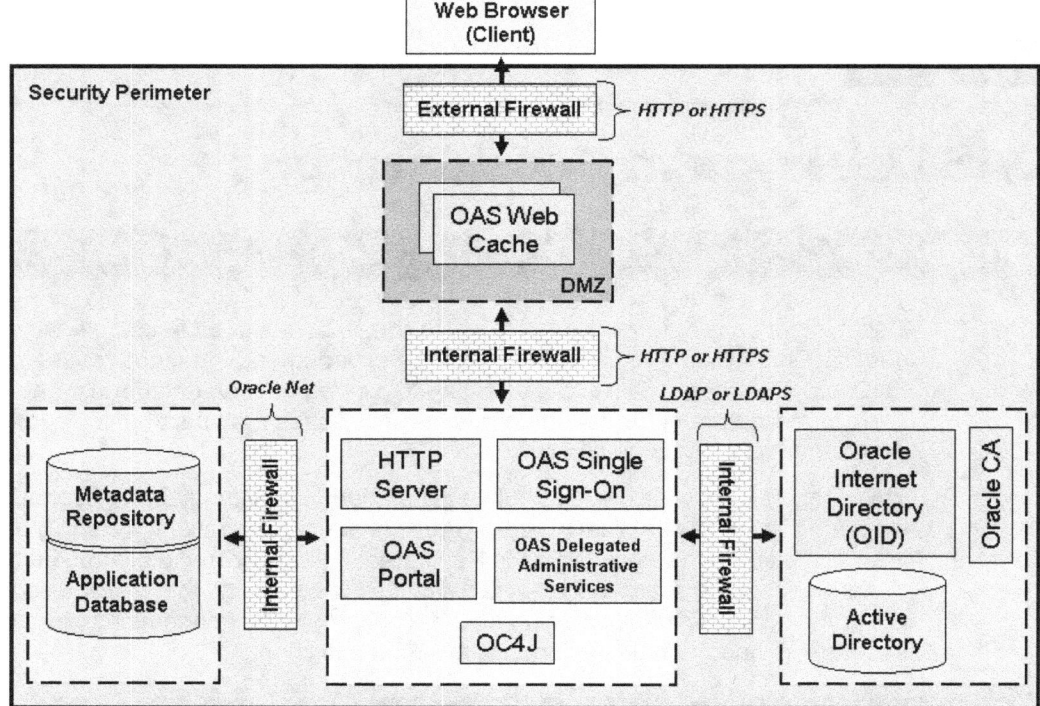

**Figure 1 OAS 10g Enterprise Deployment Strategy**

In the deployment strategy illustrated above, the internal network is partitioned into four protection zones. The least protected zone, the DMZ, is shown in red, while the most protected zones are shown in green. OAS product components are deployed into these protection zones as needed. OAS Web Cache(s) are deployed to standalone system(s) within the DMZ, while sensitive information such as user account information, X.509 certificates and so on, is deployed in zones that afford the highest level of protection.

An internal firewall deployed between two protection zones is configured to allow only the network traffic required between the protection zones. All other network traffic is blocked. Network traffic is characterized in terms of the ports and protocols that it uses. In the illustration above, firewalls deployed around the DMZ are configured to allow HTTP or HTTPS protocol, while the internal firewall that separates OID and Active Directory services from the rest of the network is configured to allow LDAP or LDAPS protocol.

The deployment of firewalls to establish protection zones within the security perimeter, and the allocation of OAS product components within those protection zones are critical security considerations governed by mission needs and applicable security policies. Deploy an external firewall and DMZ to isolate the enterprise network from the external environment. Deploy additional firewalls to provide greater protection for repositories containing sensitive data. Configure firewalls to restrict network traffic based on the protocols utilized by OAS products allocated within established protection zones.

## Platform Hardening

Platform hardening refers to the application of standardized security templates to enable and configure platform security capabilities. A variety of security templates have been developed by Microsoft, in collaboration with NSA, for Windows 2003 Server as well as other Microsoft operating systems.

Different security templates are available that provide different degrees of platform hardening. The selection of a security template is an important security consideration that depends on both the threat environment in which the system will be deployed to and the sensitivity level of the data the system will process. Recommendations on the application of NSA security templates are presented in the next chapter.

## Protecting Data in Transit

### Selective Use of SSL

There are deployment options to consider with regard to which OAS subsystems require SSL to be enabled. These considerations depend on the sensitivity of the information and the potential threat(s) the deployed system may be exposed to, as well as applicable security policies.

With OAS 10g EE, SSL is enabled independently for many OAS subsystems. Chapter 3 discusses configuration settings used to enable SSL for the OAS HTTP Server, while chapters 4 and 6 discuss configuration settings used to enable SSL with OAS Portal and LDAP, respectively.

Enabling SSL for each OAS subsystem can severely affect performance of the deployed system and may not achieve appreciable gains in securing the information. <u>Enable SSL to protect information in transit through protection zones where threats exist and where the risk of compromise is high.</u>

One approach to minimizing use of SSL is to organize content so that sensitive information is physically separated from non-sensitive information. If sensitive content is maintained separately, then it may be possible to enable SSL to protect it without forcing use of SSL to protect non-sensitive content. <u>Look for opportunities to organize content so that sensitive data can be isolated and separately protected.</u>

### Strength of Encryption

The National Institute of Science and Technology (NIST) provides guidance on the use of SSL-based cryptographic capabilities. These guidelines are summarized in the following table:

**Table 1.  NIST Cryptographic Guidelines**

| Protection Requirements | NIST Guidelines |
|---|---|
| Highest Security | *Encryption*: Advanced Encryption Standard (AES) w/ 256-bit encryption keys <br><br> *Authentication & Digest*: Digital Signature Standard (DSS) or RSA with 2048 bit keys, and Secure Hash Algorithm-1 (SHA-1) |
| Security and Performance | *Encryption*: AES w/ 128-bit encryption keys <br><br> *Authentication & Digest*: DSS or RSA w/ 1024-bit keys, and SHA-1 |
| Security and Compatibility | *Encryption*: AES w/ 128-bit encryption keys *OR* Triple Data Encryption Standard (3DES) w/ 168 or 112- bit encryption keys <br><br> *Authentication & Digest*: DSS or RSA with 1024-bit keys, and SHA-1 |

In addition, the Committee on National Security Systems (CNSS) has established guidelines for use of Advanced Encryption Standard (AES) encryption to protect National Security Information. These guidelines specify additional restrictions for systems that process classified data that include:

- Required use of AES

- Minimum key size of at least 192 bits for systems that process highly classified data.

Verify that OAS 10g EE meets applicable NIST and/or CNSS cryptographic guidelines appropriate for the enterprise environment in which the system is being deployed.

### FIPS Compliance

NIST maintains a list of evaluated products that are certified to meet FIPS 140 cryptographic requirements. Use of FIPS-certified cryptographic capabilities is required for information systems operated by the DoD and the Federal Government.

OAS 10g EE is certified to meet FIPS 140-2 cryptographic requirements. It supports SSL v3 and TLS v1 protocols, and cryptographic functions that include RC4, 3DES, and SHA-1. It is important to note that the cryptographic library bundled with OAS 10g EE does not support AES encryption. If AES is required, contact Oracle technical support for information about compatible, FIPS-certified cryptographic libraries for use with OAS 10g EE.

FIPS-certified cryptographic functions are configured to operate in FIPS compatibility mode. FIPS compatibility mode selectively enables certain cryptographic and SSL handshake/initialization functions that are allowed by FIPS 140-2. Set the SQLNET.SSLFIPS parameter in the sqlnet.ora configuration file to TRUE in order for OAS 10g EE to operate in FIPS compatibility mode.

Both Windows 2003 Server operating system and Microsoft Active Directory are certified to meet FIPS 140-2 requirements. More aggressive Microsoft security templates will reconfigure Windows 2003 Server to operate in FIPS compatibility mode. Guidance for configuring Microsoft Active Directory to operate in FIPS compatibility mode is detailed in the DISA publication "Active Directory Security Technical Implementation Guide".

### Certificate Management

An important deployment consideration is whether server side certificates alone provide adequate security. X.509 certificates are required for SSL-based encryption and certificate-based authentication. While SSL can be used without issuance of certificates to clients, SSL sessions established using only server side certificates are vulnerable to man-in-the-middle attacks. Install X.509 certificates for each server on which OAS product components are installed. In addition, install an X.509 certificate for each client if the deployment is required to utilize certificate-based authentication and/or SSL using client side certificates.

## Performance Considerations

System performance, specifically the reliability and availability of a system, is a primary security consideration for mission critical systems. A variety of deployment and configuration options affect the overall system performance of OAS 10g EE once deployed. This section discusses performance considerations using the following terminology:

- Workload – a set of inputs to be processed by the system.

- Throughput – the rate at which a system processes its workload.

- Availability – a measure of the proportion of time a system remains in a functioning state, able to process its workload.
- Scalability – the ability of a system to handle an increasing workload without compromising the throughput or availability of the system.
- Reliability – the ability of a system to perform its function when operating under hostile or unexpected conditions.

Mission-critical systems often have stringent availability requirements. Factors that contribute to a system's overall availability include the reliability and scalability of its constituent components. A component of a system whose reliability limits the reliability of the system constitutes a single point of failure for that system.

## OAS 10g EE Deployment Considerations

This section discusses deployment considerations specific to OAS 10g EE server components: OAS Web Cache, OAS HTTP Server, the OAS Portal and OAS Identity Management.

### OAS Web Cache

OAS Web Cache stores web content in memory, not to disk, making it a memory-intensive application that competes for memory resources with other software processes running on the same system. Deploy OAS Web Cache to a standalone, dedicated server to avoid potential resource conflicts with other OAS product components.

### OAS HTTP Server

OAS HTTP Server implements a plug-in architecture that supports integration of Oracle-developed or 3rd party software modules, which extend the OAS HTTP Server with additional functional capabilities. However, the more software modules installed and enabled, the greater the attack surface that the deployed system provides. Enable only Apache software modules on an OAS HTTP Server that are minimally necessary in order for the system to be mission effective. Recommendations for installation and/or removal of software modules are discussed in Chapter 3 of this security guide.

### OAS Portal

The OAS Portal provides a collaborative environment and a set of tools used by web content developers to create, maintain and publish web content. Deployment of OAS Portal is optional and may not be appropriate for production systems that are dedicated to hosting web applications or services. Verify that web content development is a mission objective before deploying web server tier system(s) with OAS Portal installed. Chapter 4 provides security recommendations in situations where OAS Portal is deployed.

### OAS Identity Management

Deployment considerations for OAS Identity Management include selection of the authoritative source for user account information, and use of clustering to ensure continuous availability of the OAS Identity Management functions.

#### Selecting the "Directory of Truth"

The "directory of truth" refers to the primary or authoritative source of user account information within the enterprise. Though user account information may be stored or modified in several locations within the enterprise, synchronization mechanisms ensure that the directory of truth and all other directories remain current and consistent.

When deploying OAS 10g EE, an important consideration is whether to use Oracle Internet Directory or an external, 3rd party LDAP service, such as Microsoft Active Directory, as the directory of truth. While no recommendations are provided in this security guide on selecting the directory of truth, this decision has important security ramifications regarding the synchronization mechanisms that must be enabled. Directory synchronization issues are discussed in Chapter 6 of this security guide.

The deployment of Microsoft Active Directory or other 3rd party, external LDAP service is not discussed in this security guide. However, deployment of OAS product components, particularly the OID, to the same host server as Microsoft Active Directory can cause resource conflicts and does not provide for physical separation between the directory of truth and other, satellite directories in which user account information resides. Regardless of which directory of truth is used, never deploy OAS product components on the same host platform as Microsoft Active Directory.

## OAS Clusters and Continuous Availability

In distributed, enterprise systems scalability and availability are managed through deployment of redundant components. OAS 10g EE implements an architectural framework called the OAS cluster, which supports coordinated processing among redundant OAS product services. An OAS cluster can be configured to operate in one of two modes, active-active or active-passive, depending on the performance and/or availability requirements that need to be satisfied.

In an OAS cluster configured in active-active mode, the workload is shared and distributed evenly across peer cluster members. Sharing the workload improves the scalability of the system and insulates users from component failures that would otherwise reduce the availability of the system. An active-active OAS cluster addresses both performance and availability issues.

In an OAS cluster configured in active-passive mode, a primary cluster member processes the workload while a secondary cluster member passively monitors the primary. Failure of the primary causes the secondary cluster member to assume the role of primary. An active-passive OAS cluster addresses availability issues only.

OAS product components, including the OAS Web Cache, OAS Portal and OAS Identity Management, can be deployed in OAS cluster configurations in order to satisfy stringent performance or availability requirements. Refer to Oracle product documentation for technical guidance on deploying OAS product components in clustered configurations.

### OAS Web Cache

A single OAS Web Cache deployed to a DMZ to intercept and forward external user requests to origin servers constitutes a single point of failure. If the OAS Web Cache becomes unavailable, users have no alternative means for routing requests through the DMZ to origin servers for processing; loss of the Web Cache renders the system unavailable to external users. Deploy multiple OAS Web Caches in a clustered configuration when high availability is required.

### OAS Identity Management

Oracle partner applications utilize OAS Identity Management capabilities to manage user account information, group memberships and the granting of privileges. Loss of availability of either the OID or the SSO Server constitutes a single point of failure that can prevent Oracle Partner applications, including Oracle administration tools, from operating. Consider deployment options that include full or partial replication of the OID directory tree and/or installation of Oracle Identity Management to redundant servers configured as an OAS cluster.

## Important Security Points

- ❑ Deploy an external firewall and DMZ to isolate the enterprise network from the external environment. Deploy additional firewalls to provide greater protection for repositories containing sensitive data. Configure firewalls to restrict network traffic based on the protocols utilized by OAS products allocated within established protection zones.

- ❑ Enable SSL to protect information in transit through protection zones where threats exist and where the risk of compromise is high.

- ❑ Look for opportunities to organize content so that sensitive data can be isolated and separately protected

- ❑ Verify that OAS 10g EE meets applicable NIST and/or CNSS cryptographic guidelines appropriate for the enterprise environment in which the system is being deployed.

- ❑ If AES is required, contact Oracle technical support for information about compatible, FIPS-certified cryptographic libraries for use with OAS 10g EE.

- ❑ Set the SQLNET.SSLFIPS parameter in the sqlnet.ora configuration file to TRUE in order for OAS 10g EE to operate in FIPS compatibility mode.

- ❑ Install X.509 certificates for each server on which OAS product components are installed. In addition, install an X.509 certificate for each client if the deployment is required to utilize certificate-based authentication and/or SSL using client side certificates.

- ❑ Deploy OAS Web Cache to a standalone, dedicated server to avoid potential resource conflicts with other OAS product components.

- ❑ Enable only Apache software modules on an OAS HTTP Server that are minimally necessary in order for the system to be mission effective.

- ❑ Verify that web content development is a mission objective before deploying web server tier system(s) with OAS Portal installed

- ❑ Never deploy OAS product components on the same host platform as Microsoft Active Directory

- ❑ Refer to Oracle product documentation for guidance on deploying OAS product components in clustered configurations.

- ❑ Deploy multiple OAS Web Caches in a clustered configuration when high availability is required.

- ❑ Consider deployment options that include full or partial replication of the OID directory tree and/or installation of Oracle Identity Management to redundant servers configured as an OAS cluster.

# OAS Installation

This chapter discusses security considerations and recommendations for installing OAS 10g EE product components on a Windows 2003 Server platform. The chapter starts with a discussion of installation considerations that apply to all tiers. This is followed by installation guidance specific to the infrastructure tier, the database tier, the web server tier and the caching tier.

Functional dependencies between OAS product components govern the order in which product components must be installed in the enterprise environment. For example, because the web server tier depends on the infrastructure tier, the infrastructure tier must be installed prior to or in combination with the web server tier. These functional dependencies are identified in the course of this chapter.

> Note: Windows administrative privileges are required in order to install OAS product components.

## Installation Considerations for All Tiers

OAS 10g EE is bundled with a wizard-based, universal product installer that presents various security-relevant configuration options for each OAS product tier. The following configuration options and installation considerations apply to all OAS product tiers.

### Oracle Installation Directories

The universal installer program installs the product into a default directory location, C:\OraHome_1, which can be reset during product installation. Throughout this security guide, %Oracle_Home% refers to the Windows 2003 Server directory in which OAS 10g EE is installed. OAS 10g EE maintains subdirectories within this installation directory that are used to store product configuration information, server logs, and so on.

The directory location where Oracle database files are physically stored can also be reset during product installation. Oracle recommends that database files be stored apart from Oracle software, on separate disks, to provide better performance. Restrict access to the Oracle installation directory, its subdirectories and the directory containing Oracle database files to administration personnel only.

### Default Port Assignments

OAS product components utilize various TCP ports to communicate with one another. These port assignments are defined in the staticports.ini template file, which is imported by the product installer during the installation process. The default port settings specified in staticports.ini are well-known, documented values. Modify default port assignments in staticports.ini prior to installing OAS.

Well-known protocols are associated with certain ports. For example, TCP port 80 is associated with the HTTP protocol. Use of default port assignments can also provide an adversary with information on the protocols being used.

Changing default port assignments does not prevent an adversary from launching attacks on a system. But it does force the adversary to perform a port scan in order to locate which ports are active and potentially exploitable. An Intrusion Detection System (IDS) can be configured to provide early warning notifications when port scans are performed. So, changing default port assignments can slow an attacker and can make their actions more visible to network security personnel.

## Installation Log Verification

The universal installer maintains a persistent log that is used to record the status of each step of the installation process. A separate installation log is created for each installation session and stored in the Program Files/Oracle/logs directory. Review installation logs to verify that OAS installed correctly. Installation errors may either cause the product to function incorrectly or disable important security capabilities.

While password information entered during the installation process is not recorded, the installation log may still provide an adversary with information that can be used to identify configuration weaknesses and potential vulnerabilities. Delete installation logs once reviewed, or restrict their access to administration personnel only.

## Enabling Security Features at Startup

The Oracle Process Manager and Notification (OPMN) service is responsible for starting OAS 10g EE product components with initial configuration settings provided the %Oracle_Home%\opmn\conf\opmn.xml configuration file.

One security-related setting in this file determines whether the OAS HTTP Server runs with SSL enabled at startup. By default, the HTTP Server runs with SSL disabled. Modify the XML start-mode attribute in the opmn.xml configuration file to ensure that SSL is enabled for the HTTP Server at startup.

## Platform Hardening

Different security templates afford different levels of protection. The selection of which security template to apply to a given platform depends on the sensitivity of the data and the threat environment in which the platform is deployed. Apply the Windows security template after OAS product components have been successfully installed.

Microsoft security templates enable Microsoft-internal firewall capabilities. This requires that Oracle applications and/or ports utilized by OAS product components be added to the firewall exception list once a template has been applied.

Security templates for Microsoft Windows Server 2003 are available from the NSA SNAC website (http://www.nsa.gov/snac/).

## Installation of the Infrastructure Tier

The infrastructure tier includes the following OAS Identity Management components: the Single Sign-On (SSO) Server, the Oracle Internet Directory (OID), Oracle Delegated Administration Services and the Oracle Certificate Authority (OCA). Installation of an external, 3rd party Certificate Authority (CA) service is not discussed in this security guide.

Some of the OAS product components listed above are functionally dependent on the Metadata Repository, which must be installed prior to or in combination with OAS Identity Management. Installation of the database tier, which includes the Metadata Repository, is discussed in the following section.

## Selecting Installation Options

By default, the universal installer installs both Identity Management and the Metadata Repository together on the same server. These components can be separately installed on servers located in different protection zones in order to provide greater isolation and protection of sensitive data stored in the Metadata Repository. Install only Oracle Identity Management when deploying the infrastructure tier into an enterprise environment where the Metadata Repository is already deployed.

In addition, the universal installer provides installation options for selectively installing certain Identity Management components, such as runtime support for OAS clusters and the Oracle Certificate Authority (OCA). Install only infrastructure tier product components that are required in order for the system to be mission effective. Installation of product features that are not required extends the attack surface of a system and can provide additional opportunities for an adversary to exploit vulnerabilities of that system.

## Installation of the Database Tier

The database tier includes application databases, database providers and the Metadata Repository. Installation of 3$^{rd}$ party, directory services such as Microsoft Active Directory is not discussed in this security guide. This guide assumes that external, 3$^{rd}$ party directory services utilized by OAS 10g EE are installed and maintained on a separate server.

OAS product components in the database tier are functionally dependent on the Oracle 10g database server, which is bundled with OAS 10g EE and installed with the Metadata Repository. The NSA, in collaboration with the Center for Internet Security (CIS), has developed a benchmark that provides guidance on configuring Oracle 10g database servers. Many of the security recommendations provided by this benchmark document may be applicable with OAS 10g EE. This document is available from the NSA SNAC website (http://www.nsa.gov/snac/).

## Selecting Installation Options

The database tier is separately installed by selecting the configuration option to install the Metadata Repository only. This option installs the Oracle 10g database, the Metadata schema and administration accounts and databases required for the product installation process.

## Resetting Default Database Passwords

The Metadata Repository includes password-protected administration accounts and databases, which are used during the installation process. Passwords for administration accounts automatically expire once installation completes. Each password must be must be reset in order to re-enable the associated administration account.

Passwords for administration databases however do not automatically expire once installation completes. The universal installer provides configuration options used to assign new passwords to these databases: SYS, SYSTEM, SYSMAN and DBSNMP. Assign strong, unique passwords for administration databases created during the installation process.

## Resetting the ias_admin Password

Each Oracle 10g database server has a separate ias_admin administration account. The universal installer provides a configuration screen that is used to reset the default ias_admin account password. Specify a strong password when setting the ias_admin account password. Guidelines for strong passwords are discussed in Chapter 6 of this security guide.

### Configuring the Oracle Database Listener

The Oracle Database Listener is a server-based process that provides network connectivity for clients, application servers, and other databases to an Oracle database. All OAS infrastructure and web server tier components access the Oracle database through the Oracle Database Listener.

By default, the Oracle Database Listener receives Oracle Net protocol messages over TCP port 1521; however, this port assignment is not specified in the staticports.ini file. As with other OAS 10g EE default port assignments, change the default port assignment for the Oracle Database Listener to obscure this well-known port-to-protocol mapping. Configuration settings for the Oracle Database Listener are located in the listener.ora configuration file in the %Oracle_Home%\network\admin directory.

TCP valid node checking is used to restrict access to the Oracle Database Listener. TCP valid node checking specifies a list of IP addresses and hostnames that are allowed to connect to the Oracle Database Listener. Restrict access to the Oracle Database Listener by enabling TCP valid node checking and by specifying IP addresses for servers that have OAS web server, portal and infrastructure tier components installed. TCP Valid Node checking is enabled through the sqlnet.ora configuration file. Configuration settings in this file include lists(s) of IP addresses or host names to be allowed or denied access to the Oracle Database Listener.

## Installation of the Web Server Tier

The web server tier, also referred to as the "middle" tier, includes the OAS HTTP Server, Oracle Containers for J2EE (OC4J), the OAS Portal, in addition to other OAS 10g EE middle tier components. This discussion assumes that these product components are being installed together on a Windows 2003 server platform, separate from infrastructure or database product components.

> Because the web server tier is functionally dependent on the infrastructure and database tiers, the web server tier is installed after installation of the infrastructure tier has been completed.

### Selecting Installation Options

Installation of the web server tier is accomplished by selecting the installation option "Oracle Application Server 10g" in the universal installer. Subsequent screens provide additional options for selectively installing the OAS Portal, OAS Wireless, Reports and Forms services and other OAS middle tier components.

As with the infrastructure tier, install only web tier product components that are required in order for the system to be mission effective. Installation of optional, unused product features can provide opportunities for an adversary to exploit vulnerabilities of a system.

### Registering with Oracle Internet Directory

The web server tier must register with the infrastructure tier in order to access the Oracle Internet Directory (OID). The universal installer provides a configuration screen that is used to perform this registration. The universal installer prompts the user to enter the OID super user password before completing this registration.

This configuration screen also provides a checkbox for enabling use of SSL to protect LDAP protocol messages. Select the configuration option "Only use SSL connections with the Oracle Internet Directory" to protect user account information transferred between OID and the web server tier via LDAP.

## Resetting Passwords for Portal Administration Accounts

Installation of OAS Portal creates accounts used for portal administration. Default passwords are assigned by the universal installer to these accounts: PORTAL, PORTAL_ADMIN and PUBLIC. Once installation is completed, assign strong passwords to all portal administration accounts. Strong passwords are described in Chapter 6 of this security guide.

## Resetting Database Access Descriptor (DAD) Passwords

Database Access Descriptors (DAD) are created during installation and contain configuration settings used by the OAS Portal to connect to Oracle databases. These configuration settings specify the database schema, assigned privileges, password, JDBC connect-string, language support settings and so on for a given database connection.

Once installation is complete, change default passwords assigned to each Database Access Descriptor (DAD) and specify strong passwords as described in Chapter 6 of this security guide.

DAD configuration settings, including passwords, are stored in the dads.conf configuration file as unencrypted values. Restrict read access to the dads.conf configuration file to administrators only.

## Restricting Access to PL/SQL Packages

PL/SQL is an Oracle-proprietary, SQL scripting language for accessing Oracle databases. PL/SQL provides access to stored procedures. However, certain PL/SQL stored procedures installed with the OAS Portal expose security vulnerabilities when they are executed through a Web browser.

Access to PL/SQL stored procedures from the OAS Portal can be denied using the PlsqlExclusionList directive. Upon installation of the OAS Portal, verify that the dads.conf configuration file excludes the following packages of PL/SQL stored procedures:

- PlsqlExclusionList sys.*
- PlsqlExclusionList dbms_*
- PlsqlExclusionList utl_*
- PlsqlExclusionList owa_util.

It is important to note that the list above is subject to change as new PL/SQL vulnerabilities are identified and existing vulnerabilities are corrected. Refer to product security updates and vendor configuration guidance for updated information regarding documented PL/SQL vulnerabilities.

## Restricting Access to the Portal Cache Directory

The OAS Portal maintains an internal cache containing assembled web pages, which is persistently stored to disk in the %Oracle_Home%/Apache/modplsql/cache directory. To prevent unauthorized access to cached portal content, configure the portal cache directory to restrict file access to cached pages.

## Installation of the Caching Tier

Deployment of the caching tier involves installation of the OAS Web Cache on one or more servers, depending on applicable availability and performance requirements. If high availability requirements exist, OAS Web Cache is installed in the DMZ on two or more servers, which are configured as an OAS Cluster. The following guidance assumes that OAS Web Cache is to be installed on a Windows 2003 Server deployed in a DMZ.

### Selecting Installation Options

Installation of a standalone OAS Web Cache is accomplished by selecting the installation option "Oracle Application Server 10g", followed by the "J2EE and Web Cache" installation type option. Even in a standalone configuration, OAS Web Cache software utilizes the OAS HTTP Server, OC4J and J2EE runtime, all of which must be installed in order for the OAS Web Cache to function.

### Registering with Oracle Internet Directory

Support for SSO-based user authentication through the OAS Web Cache requires that each OAS Web Cache be registered with the infrastructure tier.

As with the web server tier, registration of the OAS Web Cache with the infrastructure tier is performed during product installation and requires OID super user access. The universal installer prompts the user to enter the OID super user password before completing this registration. Additionally, the universal installer provides a configuration option to enable SSL to protect LDAP protocol messaging between the OAS Web Cache and the OID. Select the configuration option "Only use SSL connections with the Oracle Internet Directory" to protect user account information transferred between OID and the OAS Web Cache via LDAP.

## Important Security Points

❑ Restrict access to the Oracle installation directory, its subdirectories and the directory containing Oracle database files to administration personnel only.

❑ Modify default port assignments in staticports.ini prior to installing OAS.

❑ Review installation logs to verify that OAS installed correctly. Delete installation logs once reviewed, or restrict their access to administration personnel only.

❑ Modify the XML start-mode attribute in the opmn.xml configuration file to ensure that SSL is enabled for the HTTP Server at startup.

❑ Apply the appropriate Windows security template after OAS product components have been successfully installed.

❑ Install only Oracle Identity Management when deploying the infrastructure tier into an enterprise environment where the Metadata Repository is already deployed.

❑ Install only infrastructure tier product components that are required in order for the system to be mission effective.

❑ Assign strong, unique passwords for administration databases created during the installation process.

❑ Assign a strong password for the ias_admin administration account.

❑ Change the default port assignment for the Oracle Database Listener to obscure this well-known port-to-protocol mapping.

- ❑ Restrict access to the Oracle Database Listener by enabling TCP valid node checking and by specifying IP addresses for servers that have OAS web server, portal and infrastructure tier components installed.

- ❑ As with the infrastructure tier, install only web tier product components that are required in order for the system to be mission effective.

- ❑ Select the configuration option "Only use SSL connections with the Oracle Internet Directory" to protect user account information transferred between OID and the web server tier via LDAP.

- ❑ Once installation is completed, assign strong passwords to all portal administration accounts.

- ❑ Once installation is complete, change default passwords assigned to each Database Access Descriptor (DAD) and specify strong passwords as described in Chapter 6 of this security guide.

- ❑ Restrict read access to the dads.conf configuration file to administrators only.

- ❑ Upon installation of the OAS Portal, verify that the dads.conf configuration file excludes the following packages of PL/SQL stored procedures:

    - ■ PlsqlExclusionList sys.*

    - ■ PlsqlExclusionList dbms_*

    - ■ PlsqlExclusionList utl_*

    - ■ PlsqlExclusionList owa_util.

- ❑ Refer to product security updates and vendor configuration guidance for updated information regarding documented PL/SQL vulnerabilities.

- ❑ To prevent unauthorized access to cached portal content, configure the portal cache directory to restrict file access to cached pages.

- ❑ Select the configuration option "Only use SSL connections with the Oracle Internet Directory" to protect user account information transferred between OID and the OAS Web Cache via LDAP.

# OAS HTTP Server

## Introduction

This chapter discusses security considerations and recommendations for configuring the OAS HTTP Server. Specific topics covered in the next section include virtual hosts, installation of Apache software modules and security configuration directives applicable to OAS HTTP Server. The last section of this chapter provides a summary of important security points.

It must be noted that the Apache HTTP Server is a commonly-used open source product for which considerable security guidance already exists. The goal of this section is to focus on aspects of the Oracle-proprietary security capabilities of the OAS HTTP Server, as implemented in OAS 10g EE.

## Security Considerations

### Security Configuration of Virtual Hosts

Protection zones, security templates and OAS HTTP Server configuration settings all contribute to establishing security controls that apply uniformly to data residing on a given server. Each virtual host inherits security-related configuration settings from the OAS HTTP Server that hosts it, but can be configured to override these default configuration settings, independently from other virtual hosts running on the same server.

To minimize the use of security configuration overrides by virtual hosts, co-locate virtual hosts containing sensitive content on OAS HTTP Servers configured to protect sensitive content, and virtual hosts containing non-sensitive content on OAS HTTP Servers configured to host non-sensitive content.

Co-locating virtual hosts containing sensitive and non-sensitive content on the same physical host can result in situations where some of the content may be either under protected or over protected, depending on the security controls that are enabled. The security posture of each virtual host residing on that host must be evaluated on a case-by-case basis. In cases where the virtual host is configured to override the default security settings of the OAS HTTP Server, verify that the virtual host is configured to adequately protect its content based on the sensitivity of that content.

In cases where the virtual host does not override the default security settings of the OAS HTTP Server, verify that default OAS HTTP Server security settings are sufficient to protect the content provided by that virtual host.

### Installation of Apache Software Modules

Software modules that extend the OAS HTTP Server with product functional capabilities may introduce or expose vulnerabilities that could be exploited through the surrounding network. Several non-security software modules are installed and enabled by default during the installation process. These modules include mod_perl, mod_cgi, mod_fastcgi, mod_oradev and mod_include. <u>Disable Apache software modules that are not required</u>.

APIs used to develop Apache software modules are publicly available and are used by 3<sup>rd</sup> party developers to implement public domain extensions for the Apache HTTP server. While many of these 3<sup>rd</sup> party modules may be component compatible with OAS HTTP Server, they have not been qualified by Oracle to work with OAS 10g EE. <u>Only install and enable software modules obtained directly from Oracle.</u>

The following table lists security-related software modules bundled with the OAS HTTP Server in OAS 10g EE. As the table shows, some of these software modules are not required for correct operation of the OAS HTTP Server, while others are only available for use with Apache 1.3. Recommendations for enabling these software modules are provided after the table.

**Table 2. Security Related Apache Software Modules**

| Module Name | Required | Oracle Proprietary Module | HTTP Server Version | Purpose |
|---|---|---|---|---|
| mod_access | No | No | 1.3 and 2.0 | Controls access to the server based on hostname or IP address. |
| mod_osso | Yes | Yes | 1.3 and 2.0 | Enables Single Sign-On support for Oracle partner applications. |
| mod_auth | No | No | 1.3 and 2.0 | Optional capability that supports user authentication for Oracle external applications. |
| mod_ossl | Yes | Yes | 1.3 and 2.0 | This module replaces the OpenSSL module mod_ssl. Mod_ossl implements SSL version 3 based on Certicom and RSA technologies. |
| mod_certheaders | No | Yes | 1.3 and 2.0 | Transfers client certificate information from a reverse proxy that terminates the client SSL connection. |
| mod_proxy | Yes | No | 1.3 and 2.0 | Implements proxying capability for AJP13 (Apache JServe Protocol version 1.3), FTP, CONNECT (for SSL), HTTP 0.9, 1.0, and 1.1. |
| mod_security | No | No | Found in the 1.3, but not the 2.0 | Performs pattern matching on incoming HTTP requests, for use with enhanced logging and/or intrusion detection |

## Host and IP-based Access Control

The mod_access module restricts access to the OAS HTTP Server based on the client's hostname or originating IP address. To use this capability, lists of allowed or denied hosts are specified in the directory section of the httpd.conf configuration file. A range of IP addresses may be specified by listing them individually, or by using wildcard characters to specify an entire subnet.

Do not restrict access to content based on the IP address of the client. Use of DHCP and/or dynamic address binding by clients may render this approach ineffective if client IP addresses are subject to change. In addition, HTTP requests received through the OAS Web Cache may not specify the IP address of the originating client.

## User Authentication

The OAS HTTP Server incorporates two software modules that implement user authentication capabilities, mod_osso and mod_auth. The authentication mechanisms used depend on the application being invoked. The mod_osso module implements Single Sign-On capabilities for both Apache 1.3 and Apache 2.0-based OAS HTTP Server configurations. Enable the mod_osso software module in order for Oracle partner applications to utilize Oracle SSO authentication capabilities.

The mod_auth module is a standard Apache module that provides non-SSO, password-based authentication. Enable the mod_auth software module so that external applications, which cannot utilize SSO authentication functions, can utilize Apache-supported user authentication capabilities.

## Support for SSL and Certificate-based Authentication

The mod_ossl module provides confidentiality and authentication with X.509 client certificates over SSL. Enable the mod_ossl module in order to utilize SSL capabilities.

The mod_certheaders module is an optional, Oracle-developed module responsible for the transfer of client certification information from the OAS Web Cache, where a client's SSL connection terminates, to the OAS HTTP Server, where it is distributed to Oracle partner and external applications as an environment variable. Enable mod_certheaders if certificate-based, client authentication is performed through the OAS Web Cache.

## Proxy Support

The mod_proxy module implements request proxy capabilities used to forward client HTTP or FTP requests to other web servers on the network. This module supports both forward and reverse proxy capabilities.

As a forward proxy, the mod_proxy module redirects each request to the specified destination web server. A client browser, configured for forward proxy access, specifies the URL of the destination web server. As a reverse proxy, the mod_proxy module determines where to send each request based on the request URL. Clients are not specially configured for proxy access and do not specify, or even know, the real URL of the destination web site.

A proxy can be used to circumvent firewall protections. By default, forward proxy support in mod_proxy is disabled. If enabled, using the ProxyRequests directive, forward proxy support can provide an adversary with unrestricted access to internal web servers. Do not utilize mod_proxy with both forward and reverse proxy functions enabled at the same time. Enable forward proxy capabilities only if restrictions are defined to limit access to internal web servers.

## Intrusion Detection

The mod_security software module provides capabilities to perform pattern matching on incoming HTTP request data and to specify actions to be performed when a match occurs. The mod_security module is available as open source software from http://modsecurity.org and bundled into the OAS 10g EE product distribution for use with the Apache 1.3-based, OAS HTTP Server. When installed this module is disabled by default.

As a generalized, pattern matching, conditional action capability, mod_security has a number of potential uses when enabled in the OAS HTTP Server. For example, mod_security can be configured to record information about HTTP requests that is not available through standard OAS HTTP Server logging facilities. If configured with information about known attack signatures, mod_security module can also provide limited intrusion detection capabilities. By combining enhanced logging with intrusion detection capabilities, mod_security can augment standard Apache logging with information that can facilitate forensic analysis when a security breach occurs.

The open source version of mod_security is no substitute for a commercial-grade Intrusion Detection System (IDS), which may be required within the enterprise deployment. Unlike an open source capability, a commercial grade IDS provides automated software and/or signature updates as new attacks are discovered. Do not use the open source version of mod_security that is bundled with OAS 10g EE in lieu of commercial-grade IDS solutions.

## Protection of Audit Logs

The OAS HTTP Server maintains a persistent log of user access to web content. A separate log file is used to store each day's log records; the OAS HTTP Server automatically creates a new log at the start of each day. The capacity of each log file is constrained only by the amount of disk space available in the file system. Restrict user access to directories where OAS HTTP Server log information is physically stored in order to protect logging data from accidental or malicious modification or deletion. Recommendations for configuring the HTTP Server logging capability are discussed below.

## Security Configuration Directives

As discussed in the previous section, the OAS HTTP Server maintains configuration settings, called directives, in a number of external configuration files. These settings are loaded when the OAS HTTP Server is initialized and can be adjusted by editing the configuration file directly or through the OAS Application Server console.

Two configuration files in particular, httpd.conf and ssl.conf, are used to store security-related configuration settings that are used by the OAS HTTP Server and by virtual hosts. It is important to note that OAS HTTP Server configuration files store configuration settings as unencrypted data. Restrict access to the OAS HTTP Server configuration files httpd.conf and ssl.conf to system administrators only.

In addition, certain directives contained in these configuration files specify directory locations for OAS HTTP Server configuration information, logging data, web content and so on. Default settings for these directives are relative to the %Oracle_Home% installation directory, which is configured to restrict access to administration personnel. When changing default directory locations used by the OAS HTTP Server, verify that access permissions for the new directory locations restrict access to administration personnel.

### Security Directives in httpd.conf

The following table specifies default and recommended security configuration settings for httpd.conf. In cases where no recommended value is provided, the default (installed) value is used.

**Table 3. Httpd.conf Security Directives**

| Directive | Function | Default Value | Recommendation |
|---|---|---|---|
| Timeout | Specifies the number of seconds before server receives and sends time out. | 300 | Specify a timeout value in the range 60-120 seconds, which is adequate for most deployments. |
| ExtendedStatus | Specifies whether extended status information is recorded | | Discussed below |
| Port | Specifies the port on which the standalone server listens. | 7777 | Configure standalone HTTP Servers to listen on a port other than the default port. |
| Listen | Specifies the port that the HTTP Listener receives requests on. | 7777 | Configure the HTTP Listener to utilize a port other than the default port. |
| Directory | Specifies access controls applicable to a given directory containing web content. | | Discussed below |
| AllowOverride | Overrides standard directory access controls with access controls specified in .htaccess files. | | Discussed below |
| Allow from / Deny from | Restricts access based on client IP address or hostname | | Discussed below |
| HostnameLookups | Specifies whether the client's IP address or hostname is recorded in logging data. | Off | No change. |
| LogLevel | Specifies the amount of information to collect in the log. Range of values include: debug, info, notice, warn[ing], error, crit[ical], alert, emerg[ency]. | warn | Adjust this setting to collect more or less logging information as needed. |
| LogFormat | Specifies the format of entries in the log | | Discussed below |

| Directive | Function | Default Value | Recommendation |
|---|---|---|---|
| | file. | | |
| UseWebCacheIP | Specifies whether client IP addresses are reported to the OAS HTTP Server through the OAS Web Cache. | Discussed below | |
| ServerSignature | Specifies whether server-generated error messages contain information about the server version and host name. | On | Off – HTTP Server version information can be used by an adversary to identify potential system vulnerabilities. |

### The ExtendedStatus Directive

The ExtendedStatus directive enables collection of summary performance information on the OAS HTTP Server. This information includes:

- The running status of each child process, including the number of requests processed by each child process, the aggregate output (in bytes), and so on.

- The date and time that the server was last started.

- Statistical performance metrics, including averages for: requests per second, number of bytes output per second, number of bytes per request, and so on.

- CPU utilization per child process.

- Current request being processed by each child and its originating client host address.

The mod_status software module collects this performance information and presents the data as HTML in the form of an administration web page. This module is enabled by default.

While the above information may be of value for performance tuning the OAS HTTP Server, information about requests being processed and their originating client host addresses could be used by an adversary to attack the system. Set ExtendedStatus to Off unless required for performance tuning. If enabled, use the Allow from and Deny from directives described below to restrict access to the HTML output.

### The Directory Directive

The OAS HTTP Server restricts user access to web content based on configuration settings specified in the httpd.conf configuration file. Within this file, access restrictions to a given content directory are grouped together using the directory directive. Each directory directive specifies a file system location containing web content and contains additional directives that identify which users, groups or roles have access to the identified web content, the type of authentication required, and so on. Use the directory directive to restrict user access to file system locations containing web content, and to ensure that only authenticated users can view information contained in these directories.

## The AllowOverride Directive

The AllowOverride directive enables use of external .htaccess files, which can be used to restrict access to directories containing web content. This capability overrides access restrictions specified in the httpd.conf file using the Directory directive discussed above.

Use of .htaccess files effectively decentralizes management of configuration settings across the OAS HTTP Server. The resulting loss of centralized control over configuration settings may make the system more vulnerable to network-based attack. Do not use .htaccess files to specify access control information.

## The Allow from and Deny from Directives

The OAS HTTP Server is able to allow or restrict access based on a client's IP address or hostname. These directives, when used in conjunction with the Directory directive, allow or restrict access to file system locations containing web content.

A client IP address may be subject to change when DHCP or other form of dynamic address binding is employed on the network to which the client connects. Specify the client's hostname rather than its IP address when restricting access using the Allow from or Deny from directives.

## The LogFormat Directive

The LogFormat directive controls both the format and content of log file entries. This directive can be set to record a variety of information about each user request received and processed by the HTTP Server. At a minimum, configure the LogFormat directive so that the following information is logged for each HTTP request:

- The date and time of the request

- The host name and/or IP address of the client

- The URL accessed

For OAS HTTP Servers that host sensitive content, configure the LogFormat directive to record additional information required for periodic audit reviews and/or forensic analysis. The OAS HTTP Server can be configured to record additional information about each user request, including:

- The size (in bytes) of the HTTP request and response

- The status of all redirected requests

- The connection status once a response is sent

Logging information that is recorded but not reviewed is a waste of space. Periodically review OAS HTTP Server logs in accordance with applicable security policies.

## The UseWebCacheIP Directive

As discussed above, the minimum information logged for each HTTP request includes the IP address of the client that generates the request. For HTTP requests forwarded to the OAS HTTP Server through an OAS Web Cache, however, there are two IP addresses: the IP address of the originating client and the IP address of the server functioning as the OAS Web Cache.

The UseWebCacheIP directive instructs OAS Web Cache to forward the originating client's IP address to the OAS HTTP Server as part of the request. By default, this directive is disabled in order to avoid vulnerabilities in deployments where OAS Web Cache is not utilized. For deployments in which OAS Web Cache is running, set UseWebCacheIP to On to ensure that client IP addresses are property logged by the OAS HTTP Server.

**Security Directives in ssl.conf**

The ssl.conf configuration file contains directives used to configure the use of SSL by the OAS HTTP Server. The OAS HTTP Server functions with SSL enabled or disabled using the SSLEngine directive, discussed below, and cannot be configured to accept both HTTP and HTTPS (HTTP over SSL) requests, except through the use of virtual hosts.

The following table summarizes directives supported in the ssl.conf configuration file. Many of these directives can be applied to individual virtual hosts by declaring them within the associated `<VirtualHost>` tag. Otherwise, the directive applies globally across the HTTP Server. With these configuration directives, the directive is disabled in cases where no default value is specified.

**Table 4. Ssl.conf Security Directives**

| Directive | Function | Default Value | Recommendation |
|-----------|----------|---------------|----------------|
| SSLCARevocation File | Specifies the file where the Certificate Revocation List (CRL) is stored. | Not defined | Use the SSLCARevocationFile directive to specify the filename of the Certificate Revocation List (CRL) and assign file permissions that restrict access to administrators only. |
| SSLCARevocation Path | Specifies the directory where PEM-encoded Certificate Revocation Lists (CRLs) are stored. | Not defined | Use the SSLCARevocationPath directive to specify the file system directory where the CRL file is stored and assign directory permissions that prohibit access to all users. |
| SSLCipherSuite | Specifies the SSL cipher suite used by clients when communicating with the HTTP Server | Discussed below | |
| SSLEngine | Specifies whether SSL is enabled or disabled. | Off | Set the SSLEngine directive to On if use of SSL is required. |
| SSLLog | Specifies where the SSL engine's log file is maintained. | Not defined | Use the SSLLog directive to specify the file where SSL logging information will be stored and assign file permissions that prohibit access by all users. |

| Directive | Function | Default Value | Recommendation |
|---|---|---|---|
| SSLLogLevel | Specifies the amount of information collected in the SSL engine log. Range of values include: debug, trace, info, warn, error, none. | Not defined | Use the SSLLogLevel directive to set the logging level to collect logging information as needed. |
| SSLMutex | Specifies the type of semaphore (lock) used by SSL engine for inter-process synchronization. | none | Set the SSLMutex directive to sem to enable use of locking semaphores. |
| SSLOptions | Specifies SSL runtime options on a per-directory basis. | Not defined | With the SSLOptions directive, do not enable the FakeBasicAuth option, which allows unauthenticated access to a directory. |
| SSLPassPhraseDialog | Specifies the dialog box used for wallet access. | Builtin | |
| SSLProtocol | Specifies SSL protocol(s) for mod_ossl to use. Possible values are: SSLv2, SSLv3, TLSv1, and ALL. | ALL | Set the SSLProtocol directive to ALL – SSLv2 to disable use of SSLv2 protocol. |
| SSLRequire | Conditionally enables use of SSL at runtime, contingent on defined set of environmental or other factors. | Not defined | Do not use the SSLRequire directive to conditionally enable use of SSL. Enable use of SSL, using the SSLEngine directive, based on the sensitivity of the data. |
| SSLRequireSSL | Specifies whether clients are required to utilize SSL. | Not defined | Enable the SSLRequireSSL directive to force clients to use SSL when accessing a directory. |

| Directive | Function | Default Value | Recommendation |
|---|---|---|---|
| SSLVerifyClient | Specifies that a client must present a certificate for authentication. Valid values are: none, optional, required | Not defined | Enable the SSLVerifyClient directive if certificate-based authentication is required. |
| SSLWallet | Specifies the location of the Oracle wallet. | Not defined | Use the SSLWallet directive to specify the location of the Oracle wallet, and assign directory and file permissions to prohibit access to all users |

### The SSLCipherSuite Directive

When SSL is enabled, the SSLCipherSuite directive specifies which SSL cipher suite is to be used by clients when communicating with the OAS HTTP Server. The default value for this directive is:

ALL:!ADH:!EXPORT56:+HIGH:+MEDIUM:+LOW:+SSLv2:+EXP.

This setting is translated as follows:

- ALL enables use of all cipher suites

- !ADH disables use of Diffie-Hellman authentication

- !EXPORT56 disables use of all 56-bit export ciphers

- +HIGH enables use of ciphers that use triple DES

- +MEDIUM enables use of all ciphers with 128-bit encryption

- +LOW enables use of low strength ciphers (including single DES)

- +SSLv2 enables use of SSL version 2.0

- + EXP enables use of all export ciphers.

Set the SSLCipherSuite directive to:

ALL:!ADH:!EXPORT56:+HIGH:+MEDIUM- SSLv2 .

This modification eliminates the use of low-strength ciphers and SSLv2.

## Important Security Points

## Virtual Hosts

- ❑ To minimize the use of security configuration overrides by virtual hosts, co-locate virtual hosts containing sensitive content on OAS HTTP Servers configured to protect sensitive content, and virtual hosts containing non-sensitive content on OAS HTTP Servers configured to host non-sensitive content.

- ❑ In cases where the virtual host is configured to override the default security settings of the OAS HTTP Server, verify that the virtual host is configured to adequately protect its content based on the sensitivity of that content.
- ❑ In cases where the virtual host does not override the default security settings of the OAS HTTP Server, verify that default OAS HTTP Server security settings are sufficient to protect the content provided by that virtual host.

## Apache Software Modules

- ❑ Disable Apache software modules that are not required.
- ❑ Only install and enable software modules obtained directly from Oracle.
- ❑ Do not restrict access to content based on the IP address of the client.
- ❑ Enable the mod_osso software module in order for Oracle partner applications to utilize Oracle SSO authentication capabilities.
- ❑ Enable the mod_auth software module so that external applications, which cannot utilize SSO authentication functions, can utilize Apache-supported user authentication capabilities.
- ❑ Enable the mod_ossl module in order to utilize SSL capabilities
- ❑ Enable mod_certheaders if certificate-based, client authentication is performed through the OAS Web Cache.
- ❑ Do not utilize mod_proxy with both forward and reverse proxy functions enabled at the same time. Enable forward proxy capabilities only if restrictions are defined to limit access to internal web servers.
- ❑ Do not use the open source version of mod_security that is bundled with OAS 10g EE in lieu of commercial-grade IDS solutions.

## Directory and File Access

- ❑ Restrict user access to directories where OAS HTTP Server log information is physically stored in order to protect logging data from accidental or malicious modification or deletion.
- ❑ Restrict access to the OAS HTTP Server configuration files httpd.conf and ssl.conf to system administrators only.
- ❑ When changing default directory locations used by the OAS HTTP Server, verify that access permissions for the new directory locations restrict access to administration personnel.

## OAS HTTP Server Configuration Directives

- ❑ Use the Timeout directive to specify a timeout value in the range 60-120 seconds, which is adequate for most deployments.
- ❑ Set ExtendedStatus to Off unless required for performance tuning. If enabled, use the Allow from and Deny from directives described below to restrict access to the HTML output.
- ❑ Use the Port directive to configure standalone HTTP Servers to listen on a port other than the default port.
- ❑ Use the Listen directive to configure the HTTP Listener to utilize a port other than the default port.

- ❑ Use the Directory directive to restrict user access to file system locations containing web content and to ensure that only authenticated users can view information contained in these directories.

- ❑ Do not use .htaccess files to specify access control information.

- ❑ Specify the client's hostname rather than its IP address when restricting access using the Allow from or Deny from directives.

- ❑ At a minimum, configure the LogFormat directive so that the following information is logged for each HTTP request:
  - The date and time of the request
  - The host name and/or IP address of the client
  - The URL accessed

- ❑ For systems that host sensitive content, configure the LogFormat directive to record additional information required for periodic audit reviews and/or forensic analysis.

- ❑ Periodically review OAS HTTP Server logs in accordance with applicable security policies.

- ❑ For deployments in which OAS Web Cache is running, set UseWebCacheIP to On to ensure that client IP addresses are property logged by the OAS HTTP Server.

## OAS HTTP Server SSL Directives

- ❑ Use the SSLCARevocationFile directive to specify the filename of the Certificate Revocation List (CRL) and assign file permissions that restrict access to administrators only.

- ❑ Use the SSLCARevocationPath directive to specify the file system directory where the CRL file is stored and assign directory permissions that prohibit access to all users.

- ❑ Set the SSLCipherSuite directive to 'ALL:!ADH:!EXPORT56:+HIGH:+MEDIUM-SSLv2' to eliminate use of low-strength ciphers and SSLv2.

- ❑ Set the SSLEngine directive to On if use of SSL is required.

- ❑ Use the SSLLog directive to specify the file where SSL logging information will be stored and assign file permissions that prohibit access by all users.

- ❑ Use the SSLLogLevel directive to set the logging level to collect logging information as needed.

- ❑ Set the SSLMutex directive to sem to enable use of locking semaphores.

- ❑ With the SSLOptions directive, do not enable the FakeBasicAuth option, which allows unauthenticated access to a directory.

- ❑ Set the SSLProtocol directive to ALL –SSLv2 to disable use of SSLv2 protocol.

- ❑ Do not use the SSLRequire directive to conditionally enable use of SSL. Enable use of SSL, using the SSLEngine directive, based on the sensitivity of the data.

- ❑ Enable the SSLRequireSSL directive to force clients to use SSL when accessing a directory.

- ❑ Enable the SSLVerifyClient directive if certificate-based authentication is required.

- ❑ Use the SSLWallet directive to specify the location of the Oracle wallet, and assign directory and file permissions to prohibit access to all users.

# OAS Portal

## Introduction

This chapter discusses security considerations and recommendations for configuring the OAS Portal. Specific topics discussed in the following section include portal site security, controlling access to portal content, restricting content searches, management of portal user and group accounts and assignment of portal privileges. The last section of this chapter provides a summary of important security points.

## Security Considerations

### Portal Site Security Considerations

#### Enabling SSL

As discussed in Oracle product documentation, OAS 10g EE can be configured so that SSL is enabled throughout the OAS Portal. This configuration option enables SSL end-to-end within the web services tier by enabling SSL between each web tier component, as follows:

- HTTP over SSL between the OAS Web Cache and the OAS HTTP Server

- AJP over SSL between the OAS HTTP Server and the OAS Portal

- HTTP over SSL on the "loopback" connection from the Portal/PPE to the OAS Web Cache

Enable use of SSL throughout the OAS Portal for deployments that handle or process sensitive information.

### Controlling Access to Portal Content

The section details portal content properties used to control access. These properties are configurable through the Portal Builder application.

Table 5.  Security-Related Portal Content Properties

| Attribute Name | Description | Default Value | Recommendation |
|---|---|---|---|
| **Page Group Properties** | | | |
| Item Versioning | Specifies whether previous page items are retained when a new version is added. | none | Subject to operational requirements; no recommendation provided. |
| Display Unpublished | Specifies whether unpublished and deleted | disabled | The Manage Content privilege allows |

| Attribute Name | Description | Default Value | Recommendation |
|---|---|---|---|
| Items | items in a page are displayed when in edit mode. | | access to unpublished items while in Edit mode. Limit the granting of Manage Content privileges to Oracle users. |
| Retain deleted items | Specifies whether deleted or expired items are retained in the database | disabled | Subject to operational requirements; no recommendation provided. |
| Enable approvals and notifications | Enables portal functions that manage approvals within a page group | disabled | Enable this property for all page groups that potentially incorporate sensitive content. |
| Override page group approval process | Transfers control for managing approvals to individual page owners | disabled | Enable this property only when content published to the page group carries no risk for disclosure of sensitive information, or when content developers are qualified to perform page approvals |
| List of approvers | Specifies list of individual users or groups responsible for approving page group content | N/A | If a page approval process is enabled, ensure that the list of approvers includes qualified security review personnel. |
| Routing method for approvers | Specifies order in which approvers participate in the approval process | One at a time, all must approve | Subject to operational requirements; no recommendation provided. |
| **Page Properties** | | | |
| Display Page to Public Users | Marks the portal page as PUBLIC. | disabled | Enable this property only when content published to the page carries no risk for disclosure of sensitive information. |
| Enable Item Level Security | Specifies that each page item defines its own access restrictions | disabled | Discussed below |
| **Page Item Properties** | | | |
| Grant Access | Specifies the list of users | Page owner and | Discussed below |

| Attribute Name | Description | Default Value | Recommendation |
|---|---|---|---|
| | and groups granted access to the page item | page item creator | |
| Publish date | Specifies the date when the page item is available | N/A | N/A |
| Expiration period | Specifies how long before the page item is marked as expired | 30-days | Set the expiration period of a page item to be consistent with the volatility of the information it contains. Continued publication of expired or out-of-date information diminishes the integrity of the system. |

## Page Properties: Enable Item Level Security

Enabling item level security allows a content developer to grant access to individual page items that comprise a page. This capability can be used, for example, to produce a web page that grants read access to all fields, but write access to a selected subset of fields based on the accessing user's identity or group affiliation.

When item level security is enabled, each page item is independently configured to inherit the access controls assigned to the web page or tab that contains the page item, or to restrict access based on the grant access page item property, discussed below.

The functional capabilities provided by a portal page determine which users, groups and roles will use it, and which page items it must contain. This analysis is an integral part of portal content development, which is out of scope for this security guide. From a security perspective, however, occasional use of item level security is appropriate for portal pages that implement functions performed by different administration groups or roles. Do not enable item level security for a portal page if that page implements functions intended exclusively for a single user, group or functional role.

## Page Item Properties: Grant Access

The grant access page item property defines an ACL that specifies users, groups or roles that have access to the page item, with access defined in terms of available Portal page-item privileges, View, Edit and Manage.

An ACL specified in terms of groups or roles, instead of individual users, is easiest to create and maintain. Assigned privileges are associated with named roles. Users are added to or removed from a named role based on the privileges required. Create functional groups or roles that grant page item read or write access. Assign user membership to these functional groups based on the level of privileges that they require.

The Manage item privilege grants the ability to read, write and delete a page item from a page. This privilege also allows a user to modify the page item's ACL. By default, this privilege is available to the page owner and the page item creator. Limit the granting of the manage page item privilege to Oracle users other than the page owner and page item creator

## Restricting Content Searches

### Oracle Ultra Search

Oracle Ultra Search implements a secure search capability, which returns content that satisfies specified search criteria AND that the user is allowed to view. An Access Control List (ACL) can be defined that specifies which users or groups have read access to a given document or data source.

The Ultra Search crawler can be configured to search data sources that include OAS Portal page groups. With portal content, however, it is not possible to assign separate ACLs to individual web pages. Instead, the ACL is defined for the data source and applies to each web page published to that page group.

In order for the crawler to search portal content, a data source must be created for each portal page group and registered with the Ultra Search engine. This is performed as an Ultra Search administrative function. It is important to note that Oracle Ultra Search only returns portal pages that are marked PUBLIC.

To restrict access to content through Oracle Ultra Search, assign an ACL to each data source and specifies only those users and groups for which access is granted.

## Management of Portal User and Group Accounts

OAS 10g EE incorporates Role Based Access Control (RBAC) capabilities that are based on pre-defined, default functional roles and operational privileges. In addition to default (seeded) user and group accounts, the OAS Portal supports facilities that allow for self-registration of portal users, with adjudicated assignment of privileges to portal users.

### Pre-defined Portal User and Group Accounts

OAS Portal is installed with a set of pre-defined administration user and group accounts. These user and group accounts are necessary to ensure correct operation of the OAS Portal, as well as other OAS product components. Appendix B includes a list of pre-defined OAS Portal user and group accounts.

Assign strong passwords to pre-defined OAS Portal administration accounts. Limit access to Portal administration passwords, and limit user membership in OAS Portal administration groups such as DBA and PORTAL_ADMINISTRATORS.

### Portal User Self-Registration

By default, the OAS Portal is configured with portal user self-registration capabilities disabled. In this configuration, each new portal user account is explicitly created by a portal administrator using the Portal Builder application.

The self-registration feature can be enabled by a portal administrator through the Portal Builder application. Configuration options are used to specify a registration approval process, in which registration requests are forwarded to one or more portal administrators for review. The approval process specifies one or more portal administrators and a routing method indicating whether approval requires concurrence by one or by all.

Unrestricted portal user self-registration is not appropriate when portal content includes sensitive data. If portal user self-registration is enabled, ensure that an approval process is established to evaluate registration requests relative to need-to-know access restrictions that are being enforced.

## Assignment of OAS Portal Privileges

Fine grained privileges can be assigned to ensure that users possess only those privileges required in order to perform their assigned functions. This is consistent with the principal of least privilege. At the same time, the right combinations of privileges must be granted so that a user, operating in a particular functional role, has all the privileges needed to perform the duties associated with that role. Appendix B contains a list of available Portal privileges.

Pre-defined OAS Portal administration accounts are assigned default group memberships that convey administrative privileges. <u>Review the set of privileges assigned to each Portal user and administration account to ensure that the right combination of privileges is being granted.</u>

### Restricted Granting of Global Privileges

Global privileges are granted to a user or group and apply across all objects of a given type. For example, if the Manage Content Page privilege is assigned as a global privilege, it grants the user the ability to add, edit, hide or show all pages maintained by the OAS Portal. <u>Limit and periodically review the granting of global privileges to OAS Portal users.</u>

## Important Security Points

- ❑ Enable use of SSL throughout the OAS Portal for deployments that handle or process sensitive information.
- ❑ Limit the granting of Manage Content privileges to Oracle users.
- ❑ Enable the Approvals and Notifications page group property for all page groups that potentially incorporate sensitive content.
- ❑ Enable the Override Approval Process page group property only when content published to the page group carries no risk for disclosure of sensitive information, or when content developers are qualified to perform page approvals.
- ❑ If a page approval process is enabled, ensure that the list of approvers includes qualified security review personnel.
- ❑ Enable the Display Page to Public page property only when content published to the page carries no risk for disclosure of sensitive information.
- ❑ Do not enable item level security for a portal page if that page implements functions intended exclusively for a single user, group or functional role.
- ❑ Create functional groups or roles that grant page item read or write access. Assign user membership to these functional groups based on the level of privileges that they require.
- ❑ Limit the granting of the manage page item privilege to Oracle users other than the page owner and page item creator.
- ❑ Set the expiration period of a page item to be consistent with the volatility of the information it contains. Continued publication expired or out-of-date information diminishes the integrity of the system.
- ❑ To restrict access to content through Oracle Ultra Search, assign an ACL to each data source and specifies only those users and groups for which access is granted.
- ❑ Assign strong passwords to pre-defined OAS Portal administration accounts. Limit access to Portal administration passwords, and limit user membership in OAS Portal administration groups such as DBA and PORTAL_ADMINISTRATORS.
- ❑ If portal user self-registration is enabled, ensure that an approval process is established to evaluate registration requests relative to need-to-know access restrictions that are being enforced.

❑ Review the set of privileges assigned to each Portal user and administration account to ensure that the right combination of privileges is being granted.

❑ Limit and periodically review global privileges granted to OAS Portal users.

# OAS Web Cache

## Introduction

This chapter discusses security considerations and recommendations for configuring the OAS Web Cache. Specific topics covered in the next section include confidentiality of cached content, caching of sensitive and dynamic content, and effects of caching on performance. The last section of this chapter provides a summary of important security points.

## Security Considerations

### Exceptions to Previous Recommendations

Located within the DMZ, an OAS Web Cache accepts and forwards HTTP requests from external users to origin servers located within the enterprise network. When deployed as a standalone system, OAS Web Cache is installed with OAS HTTP Server and the J2EE runtime environment. Consequently, many of the security recommendations discussed in Chapter 3 for configuring OAS HTTP Server also apply the OAS Web Cache.

One exception to this is guidance regarding forward proxy support in the HTTP Server. The OAS Web Cache functions exclusively as a reverse proxy, which evaluates and forwards HTTP requests to origin servers transparently to the user. Enabling forward proxy support within a DMZ would provide external users and potential adversaries with a capability to probe systems in the DMZ or elsewhere on the enterprise network.

### Conveying User Identity Information through the OAS Web Cache

User access to web content hosted by an OAS HTTP Server is based on configuration directives such as the Directory directive, which grants or denies access based on the user's identity, client hostname or IP address.

A user's identity is established by the user authentication process. The OAS Web Cache can be configured to force external clients to perform certificate-based authentication. Governing security policies may require user authentication based on client certificates. If so, configure the OAS Web Cache to require client-side certificates.

Because no direct connection exists between the external user and the origin server, OAS product components must be configured to forward user identity information received by the OAS Web Cache to the OAS HTTP Server where it is used to mediate access.

As discussed in Chapter 3, Apache software modules and OAS HTTP Server directives are configured to enable the exchange of user identification information. In the origin OAS HTTP Server, the mod_certheaders software module is enabled so that client certificate information can be received from the OAS Web Cache. In addition, the UseWebCacheIP directive is enabled so that the external client's IP address is included in HTTP requests forwarded by the OAS Web Cache.

Both configuration settings are disabled by default because they expose potential security vulnerabilities when enabled in the absence of the OAS Web Cache. Verify that OAS Web Cache and OAS HTTP Server are configured to accept and receive IP address and/or client certificate information from external users, as required.

## Protecting the Confidentiality of Content through the OAS Web Cache

The confidentiality of sensitive content returned by an origin server to an external user through the OAS Web Cache is not protected end-to-end by a single SSL session. The delivery of content to an external user involves two separate data transfers: Content is transferred from an origin server to the OAS Web Cache, where it is stored. Once stored, content is delivered to the external user by the OAS Web Cache.

Depending on the sensitivity of the content and governing security policies, SSL may be required to protect content over one or both legs of this information flow. If sensitive content is delivered through the OAS Web Cache, enable use of SSL between the OAS Web Cache and external users.

While enabling use of SSL between the OAS Web Cache and an origin server can seriously affect system throughput, it is an effective mitigation for insider threats. Governing security policies may require end-to-end protection for highly sensitive data transferred within the enterprise network. Consider the tradeoff between throughput performance and the need to protect sensitive content transferred between each origin server and the OAS Web Cache, on a case-by-case basis.

OAS Web Cache is configured with information about origin servers through the OAS Web Cache management console, through which each origin server is defined by its IP address, its port, and whether HTTPS protocol provides the underlying transport. Enable use of HTTPS when configuring the OAS Web Cache to access an origin server that provides sensitive content, or when governing security policies require end-to-end protection of data as a mitigation strategy for insider threats.

### Caching of Sensitive Content

The OAS Web Cache maintains an in memory cache of web content returned to external users in response to their requests. While the size of this memory cache is an OAS Web Cache configuration option, the amount of content stored in the memory cache at any given time is determined by caching and invalidation rules, the volume of user requests and the garbage collection mechanism, which purges content when the cache size limit is reached.

The OAS Web Cache does not isolate or protect cached content based on its sensitivity. Content received from an origin server over a HTTP session is not isolated, within the OAS Web Cache, from sensitive content received from an origin server over a HTTPS session.

An OAS Web Cache is deployed in a DMZ, which is most exposed region of an enterprise network. Sensitive content cached by an OAS Web Cache deployed in a DMZ may be subject to continual, systematic attack and possible compromise by adversaries located outside of the enterprise. If the OAS Web Cache is configured to cache both sensitive and non-sensitive content, regard all cached data as sensitive content stored in a high threat environment.

It is possible to set restrictions on the ability of the OAS Web Cache to cache sensitive content. A caching rule can specify a caching policy of "Don't Cache" and a URL path prefix, which identifies an origin server that contains sensitive content. When an external user requests content, the request is forwarded to the origin server to be processed. The sensitive content is returned to the external user through the OAS Web Cache, but this caching rule prevents the content from being added to the cache. Configure the OAS Web Cache with caching rules to restrict caching of sensitive information.

In addition to caching rules, content can include HTTP header directives that specify caching restrictions. For example, the Single Sign-On (SSO) Server login and logout web pages both contain HTTP Surrogate-Control: no_store header directives, which prevent caching in the OAS Web Cache. Unlike a caching rule, which may specify an entire content directory on an origin server, an HTML header directive applies only to the content page that contains it.

It is important to note however that the HTTP Surrogate-Control: no_store header directive overrides caching and expiration rules that would otherwise apply to a given web page. This override ensures that content marked with the no_store directive, such as the SSO Server login page, can never be cached. <u>Verify that the use of HTTP Surrogate-Control header directives is consistent with security policies for restricting the caching of sensitive content.</u>

## Caching of Dynamic Content

When dynamic content is cached, a potential exists for stale content to be delivered in response to a user request. Stale content refers to cached web content that is out-of-sync with content that would be returned by the origin server if it were processing the request directly. As an example, a cached "calendar" web page that reports the current date would become stale after 24 hours has elapsed.

Stale content is a data integrity issue. Deployments that host mission critical applications may regard stale content to be unacceptable. Without any caching rules defined, OAS Web Cache will only cache static content, which never goes stale. <u>If caching of dynamic content is required, define expiration rules that establish expiration timeframes consistent with the volatility of the content.</u> For the calendar page example above, an expiration rule that sets the page to expire within 24 hours of when it was created would prevent that page from becoming stale.

It is also possible to control the caching and expiration of dynamic content using HTTP Surrogate-Control (SC) header directives, which override caching and expiration rules defined in the OAS Web Cache. <u>Verify that the use of SC header directives in web pages containing dynamic content is consistent with security policies that define enterprise data integrity requirements regarding access to stale dynamic content.</u>

## Important Security Points

- ❏ Governing security policies may require user authentication based on client certificates. If so, configure the OAS Web Cache to require client-side certificates.

- ❏ Verify that OAS Web Cache and OAS HTTP Server are configured to accept and receive IP address and/or client certificate information from external users, as required.

- ❏ If sensitive content is delivered through the OAS Web Cache, enable use of SSL between the OAS Web Cache and external users.

- ❏ Consider the tradeoff between throughput performance and the need to protect sensitive content transferred between each origin server and the OAS Web Cache, on a case-by-case basis.

- ❏ Enable use of HTTPS when configuring the OAS Web Cache to access an origin server that provides sensitive content, or when governing security policies require end-to-end protection of data as a mitigation strategy for insider threats.

- ❏ If the OAS Web Cache is configured to cache both sensitive and non-sensitive content, regard all cached data as sensitive content stored in a high threat environment.

- ❏ Configure the OAS Web Cache with caching rules to restrict caching of sensitive information.

- ❏ Verify that the use of HTTP Surrogate-Control header directives is consistent with security policies for restricting the caching of sensitive content.

- ❏ If caching of dynamic content is required, define expiration rules that establish expiration timeframes consistent with the volatility of the content.

- ❏ Verify that the use of HTTP Surrogate-Control header directives in web pages containing dynamic content is consistent with security policies that define enterprise data integrity requirements regarding access to stale dynamic content.

# OAS Identity Management

## Introduction

This chapter discusses security considerations and recommendations for configuring the OAS Identity Management. Specific topics covered in the next section include password policy management, secure synchronization between OID and Microsoft Active Directory, configuring OID security, administrative access, and group, roles and user account administration. The last section of this chapter provides a summary of important security points.

## Security Considerations

### Password Policy Management

OAS Identity Management provides administrative capabilities for enforcing use of strong passwords, for managing password lockouts and for restricting password lifecycles.

#### Guidelines for "Strong" Passwords

Guidelines for strong passwords are intended to reduce the likelihood that an adversary can guess or otherwise deduce a user's password. NIST and NSA guidelines for strong passwords include the following:

- Use a minimum length of 8-12 characters,
- Include characters from at least 3 of the following:
    - upper case letters
    - lower case letters
    - numbers
    - special characters including !,@,#,$ and %.

OAS Identity Management provides limited capabilities for enforcing the above guidelines. Specifically, no capability is provided to enforce use of upper or lower case letters, or special characters.

With OAS 10g EE, password policy management capabilities can be extended with a custom-developed, password plug-in module that can impose additional validation restrictions for passwords. Refer to Oracle product documentation for information on developing custom plug-in password validation modules.

#### Password Lockout and Lifecycle Management

Password lockout management includes controls that govern how OAS 10g EE handles occasions when a system user incorrectly enters a password. OAS Identify Management provides administrative controls that specify the number of incorrect logins allowed before a user account becomes locked, how long user account remains locked, the time delay between successive login attempts, and so on.

Password lifecycle management includes controls that govern when a password reset is required. OAS Identity Management provides administrative controls that establish the expiration period for a given password, and the number of past passwords retained to ensure historical uniqueness.

The following table lists default and recommended values for password policy settings supported by OAS Identity Management. These settings are configurable through the Oracle Directory Manager tool, discussed below.

**Table 6.  OAS 10g EE Password Policy Settings**

| Policy Setting | Default Value | Recommended Value |
|---|---|---|
| Enable OID Password Policy | Enabled | Enabled |
| Need to Supply Original Password when Modifying Password | Disabled | Enabled |
| Number of Grace Logins after Password Expiration | None | None |
| Password Expiration Warning | 3 days | 3 days |
| Password Expiry Time | 60 days | NSA security templates specify a standard password expiration period of 42 days. |
| Reset Password upon next Login | Disabled. | Use this control to periodically force all users to reset account passwords. |
| Use reversible encryption | Disabled | Enable this feature only when synchronization between OID and Active Directory requires exchange of user password information. |
| Global Lockout Duration | 1 day | NSA security templates specify a standard lockout period of 15 minutes to prevent dictionary attacks. |
| Password Failure Count Interval | 0 – resets count upon successful authentication. | No change |
| Password Maximum Failure | 10 attempts | 3 attempts |
| IP Lockout Duration | Disabled. | Same as Global Lockout Duration. |

| IP Lockout Maximum Failure | Disabled | Same as Password Maximum Failure. |
|---|---|---|
| Minimum Number of Characters in Password | Minimum 5 characters. | Minimum 8-12 characters; use longer passwords when processing sensitive data. |
| Number of Numeric Characters in Password | Minimum 1 numeric character | In the absence of capabilities to enforce use of uppercase, lowercase and/or special characters in passwords, increase the minimum to 3 numeric characters. |
| Number of Password in History | None. | NSA security templates specify a standard history size of 24 passwords. |

## Synchronization between OID and Active Directory

### Configuring Export Connector Profiles

Export connectors are used to export OID user account information to Active Directory. A sample export connector profile called ActiveExport in provided in OAS 10g EE. This profile defines the mapping between directory tree attributes stored in OID and directory tree attributes stored in Active Directory. This default profile is modified in order to specify the subset of directory tree attributes to export from OID to Active Directory during the synchronization process. Verify that the export connector profile omits from its mapping all sensitive OID user account attributes that are not intended to be exported to Active Directory.

### Enabling Secure LDAP

Selection of the directory of truth is an important deployment consideration that determines which synchronization mechanism, either DirSync or uSNChanged, must be enabled. Regardless of the synchronization method selected, LDAP serves as the underlying transport protocol used to transfer user account information between OID and Active Directory. Enable secure LDAP to protect user account data being synchronized between OID and Microsoft Active Directory.

A secure LDAP session between OID and Active Directory requires both parties to utilize strong, mutual authentication during SSL session setup. Hence, both OID and Active Directory each require an X.509 certificate for authentication purposes. Verify that valid X.509 certificates are installed in the Microsoft domain controller that is hosting the Active Directory service, which OID is to synchronize with, and in the Oracle Wallet utilized by with Oracle Directory Integration and Provisioning (DIP) service.

### Synchronizing Password Values

Microsoft Active Directory stores passwords as hashed values using a Microsoft-proprietary hashing function called Unicode, which is not supported by Oracle. Because OID and AD do not support a common hashing function, it is necessary to synchronize actual password values, instead of password hashes.

To achieve this, Oracle password policy management provides a configuration setting that is used to enable user password reversible encryption. This configuration setting causes OID to store password values in an encrypted format that can be decrypted by the Oracle DIP server during the synchronization process. When this option is enabled, password values are exchanged in the clear over LDAP. Enable secure LDAP if password reversible encryption is utilized.

## Configuring OID Security

### Restricting Access to OID Administration Tools

OID administration tools are installed in the "%Oracle_Home%\ldap" directory, and include both command line tools and the Oracle Directory Manager, which is a java-based administration tool. Unrestricted access to these tools constitutes a significant security risk. Verify that Windows directory permissions restrict access to OID management tools to Windows administration personnel.

### Enabling OID Directory Auditing

With directory auditing, audit trail data is collected as OID directory information changes. The OID Directory Manager tool is used to configure directory auditing and to control the amount of audit data collected. To configure OID auditing to monitor the system for unauthorized access, enable the following OID audit configuration options:

- Superuser login

- Bind unsuccessful

- Access Violation

When directory auditing is enabled, periodically review audit data generated by the Oracle Directory Manager tool.

### Blocking Anonymous Access

By default, OID supports anonymous binding, in which an unauthenticated user is able to view OID directory data using 3rd party LDAP directory browsing tools. Using anonymous binding, user account and group membership information can be harvested from the OID.

While OID access can be restricted using Access Control Lists (ACLs), discussed below, a more effective and secure approach is to explicitly disable all anonymous binding by LDAP directory browsing tools. Use the Oracle Directory Manager tool to configure OID to disable anonymous binding.

### Protecting OID Data using Access Control Lists (ACLs)

Oracle 10g EE supports capabilities to restrict access to OID data using directory Access Control Lists (ACLs). A directory ACL is associated with a given OID subtree and specifies what types of access are allowed for a given user or application.

Using directory ACLs, it is possible to grant or deny user access to the entire OID repository, a subtree or a leaf attribute. The directory ACL can specify users by their Distinguished Name (DN) identifiers and the mode(s) of access allowed, such as right to bind, right to search, right to read, right to write and so on.

Directory ACLs must be configured to support synchronization between OID and Microsoft Active Directory. The grantrole.ldif configuration file is used to configure directory ACLs to allow OID synchronization with Microsoft Active Directory. Apply the grantrole.ldif configuration file when configuring OID 10g EE to synchronize user account data with Microsoft Active Directory.

The Oracle Directory Manager tool provides capabilities to inspect and modify directory ACLs. However, given the complex nature of OID directory storage and Oracle-defined privileges, modification of directory ACLs by hand can introduce serious security vulnerabilities. <u>Limit use of the Oracle Directory Manager tool for modifying OID directory ACLs.</u>

## Web-Based Administrative Access

Sensitive information includes system configuration and user account information, such as administration passwords. Use of SSL is an effective way to secure this sensitive information.

OAS 10g EE includes several, pre-defined web pages used to manage product configuration information, including the OAS Administration console, the OID self-service console, the Single Sign-On (SSO) Server homepage, plus web pages used to edit SSO server configuration information, administer Oracle Partner and external applications, and so on. These administration web pages require authenticated access and solicit the user to provide sensitive user account information such as an administration password. As administration web pages, they also display sensitive product configuration information and/or provide capabilities for modifying product configuration information. <u>Verify that SSL is enabled for OAS administration web pages,</u> especially web pages used to configure the SSO Server or Oracle partner applications and/or to access OID user account data.

## Administration Groups, Roles and User Accounts

Access to administrative functions through web pages and other OAS 10g EE tools is granted to predefined Oracle administration groups, roles and administration user accounts, where the level of privilege determines which functions are available to the user once authenticated.

### Global, Realm and End User Administration Groups

Administration groups are organized in a hierarchical (tree) structure. The root of this tree structure constitutes the global administration group, which conveys system-wide, administrative privileges over all Oracle users.

Realm administration groups constitute the next level in this tree structure. A realm is defined as a uniquely-named collection of Oracle users for which a particular set of security policies is enforced. A realm administration group conveys administrative privileges to all Oracle users that comprise the realm.

The lowest level in the privilege hierarchy consists of user and group level privileges, which convey minimal administrative capabilities through the Delegated Administration Service (DAS), beyond user self-service administration and group membership management.

<u>Restrict and periodically review user membership in Oracle administration groups, especially global and realm administration groups, which may grant authority over significant numbers of Oracle users.</u>

Appendix A includes a list of pre-defined Oracle administration groups and roles.

### Pre-defined Administration Roles

A role is a collection of privileges that is granted and revoked as a unit. An Oracle user can be assigned to a role and thereby granted the privileges associated with that role. Administration roles possess privileges required to perform administrative functions.

With all groups and roles, user membership is dynamic. OAS 10g EE includes a collection of pre-defined administration roles and provides capabilities for creating and managing new roles.

Creation of a new role involves assignment of an initial set of privileges to a group, followed by elevation of that group to a role. Role creation and the assignment of Oracle users to designated roles are performed through OAS Portal administrative functions.

Verify that pre-defined administration roles meet operational requirements of the target deployment. If a new role must be created, make sure that only the minimum set of privileges required for that role is granted to it. Periodically review the assignment of Oracle users to roles that grant administrative privileges.

Appendix A includes a list of pre-defined Oracle administration groups and roles.

### Pre-defined User and Administration Accounts

Oracle 10g EE installs with a number of pre-defined administration accounts, which are used to gain administrative access to the system. Correct operation of the product depends on use of pre-defined administration accounts, which have assigned privileges necessary to perform various administrative functions.

Pre-defined administration accounts cannot be deleted or renamed. Removal of privileges assigned to these accounts may degrade capabilities to effectively administer the system. Given this, it is imperative that predefined Oracle accounts be protected from unauthorized use. Assign strong passwords to pre-defined Oracle administration accounts. Restrict access to administration password information and take steps to prevent its unauthorized disclosure.

It may be feasible to disable pre-defined Oracle administration accounts that are used to administer OAS 10g EE product components that are not installed or used. For example, if OAS Portal is not installed, disable the PORTAL and PORTAL_ADMIN administration accounts to reduce the risk of unauthorized users gaining administrative access. Administration accounts are disabled by setting the OID orclisenabled attribute to disabled through the OID Directory Management tool.

Appendix A includes a list of pre-defined Oracle user and administration accounts.

## Important Security Points

- ❑ Enable password policy settings to require a user to supply their original password when changing their password.

- ❑ Set the Password Expiry Time to 42 days, which is the standard password expiration period defined in NSA/Windows security templates.

- ❑ Use the Reset Password upon Next Login policy setting to periodically force users to reset account passwords.

- ❑ Enable the Use Reversible Encryption password policy setting only when synchronization between OID and Microsoft Active Directory requires exchange of user password information.

- ❑ Set the Global Lockout Duration and IP Lockout Duration password policy settings to 15 minutes, which is the standard lockout period defined in NSA/Windows security templates.

- ❑ Reduce the Password Maximum Failure and IP Lockout Maximum Failure password policy settings from 10 attempts to 3 attempts.

- ❑ Set the Minimum Number of Characters in Password policy setting to a value between 8 and 12 characters; use longer passwords in deployments where sensitive data is processed.

- In the absence of capabilities that enforce use of uppercase and/or special characters in passwords, increase the Number of Numeric Characters in Password policy setting from 1 numeric character to 3 numeric characters.

- Set the Number of Passwords in History policy setting to 24 passwords, which is the standard history length defined in NSA/Windows security templates.

- Verify that the export connector profile omits from its mapping all sensitive OID user account attributes that are not intended to be exported to Active Directory.

- Enable secure LDAP to protect user account data being synchronized between OID and Microsoft Active Directory.

- Verify that valid X.509 certificates are installed in the Microsoft domain controller that is hosting the Active Directory service, which OID is to synchronize with, and in the Oracle Wallet utilized by with Oracle Directory Integration and Provisioning (DIP) service.

- Enable secure LDAP if password reversible encryption is utilized.

- Verify that Windows directory permissions restrict access to OID management tools to Windows administration personnel.

- To configure OID auditing to monitor the system for unauthorized access, enable the following OID audit configuration options:

  - Superuser login

  - Bind unsuccessful

  - Access Violation

- When directory auditing is enabled, periodically review audit data generated by the Oracle Directory Manager tool.

- Use the Oracle Directory Manager tool to configure OID to disable anonymous binding.

- Apply the grantrole.ldif configuration file when configuring OID 10g EE to synchronize user account data with Microsoft Active Directory.

- Limit use of the Oracle Directory Manager tool for modifying OID directory ACLs.

- Verify that SSL is enabled for OAS administration web pages, especially web pages used to configure the SSO Server or Oracle partner applications, or to access OID user account data.

- Restrict and periodically review user membership in Oracle administration groups, especially global and realm administration groups, which may grant authority over significant numbers of Oracle users.

- Verify that pre-defined administration roles meet operational requirements of the target deployment. If a new role must be created, make sure that only the minimum set of privileges required for that role is granted to it. Periodically review the assignment of Oracle users to roles that grant administrative privileges.

- Assign strong passwords to pre-defined Oracle administration accounts. Restrict access to administration password information and take steps to prevent its unauthorized disclosure.

- If OAS Portal is not installed, disable the PORTAL and PORTAL_ADMIN administration accounts to reduce the risk of unauthorized users gaining administrative access.

# Summary of Security Points

## Overview

- ❏ For performance reasons, use of encryption to protect public or unclassified data may not be justified.

- ❏ For sensitive data, use of SSL can be an effective mitigation for many common communications vulnerabilities.

- ❏ Select cryptographic algorithms and encryption key sizes based on the sensitivity of the data that must be protected.

- ❏ Develop or deploy Oracle Partner applications, which can take advantage of Oracle identity management capabilities for storing and managing password information.

- ❏ Enforce "strong" authentication using client-side certificates for systems that process highly sensitive data.

- ❏ Restrict the role and group membership of each user account, especially standard Oracle user accounts created during product installation.

- ❏ Practice the principle of least privilege when assigning permissions to new administration groups or roles.

## OAS Deployment Considerations

- ❏ Deploy an external firewall and DMZ to isolate the enterprise network from the external environment. Deploy additional firewalls to provide greater protection for repositories containing sensitive data. Configure firewalls to restrict network traffic based on the protocols utilized by OAS products allocated within established protection zones.

- ❏ Enable SSL to protect information in transit through protection zones where threats exist and where the risk of compromise is high.

- ❏ Look for opportunities to organize content so that sensitive data can be isolated and separately protected

- ❏ Verify that OAS 10g EE meets applicable NIST and/or CNSS cryptographic guidelines appropriate for the enterprise environment in which the system is being deployed.

- ❏ If AES is required, contact Oracle technical support for information about compatible, FIPS-certified cryptographic libraries for use with OAS 10g EE.

- ❏ Set the SQLNET.SSLFIPS parameter in the sqlnet.ora configuration file to TRUE in order for OAS 10g EE to operate in FIPS compatibility mode.

- ❏ Install X.509 certificates for each server on which OAS product components are installed. In addition, install an X.509 certificate for each client if the deployment is required to utilize certificate-based authentication and/or SSL using client side certificates.

- ❑ Deploy OAS Web Cache to a standalone, dedicated server to avoid potential resource conflicts with other OAS product components.
- ❑ Enable only Apache software modules on an OAS HTTP Server that are minimally necessary in order for the system to be mission effective.
- ❑ Verify that web content development is a mission objective before deploying web server tier system(s) with OAS Portal installed
- ❑ Never deploy OAS product components on the same host platform as Microsoft Active Directory
- ❑ Refer to Oracle product documentation for guidance on deploying OAS product components in clustered configurations.
- ❑ Deploy multiple OAS Web Caches in a clustered configuration when high availability is required.
- ❑ Consider deployment options that include full or partial replication of the OID directory tree and/or installation of Oracle Identity Management to redundant servers configured as an OAS cluster.

## OAS Installation

- ❑ Restrict access to the Oracle installation directory, its subdirectories and the directory containing Oracle database files to administration personnel only.
- ❑ Modify default port assignments in staticports.ini prior to installing OAS.
- ❑ Review installation logs to verify that OAS installed correctly. Delete installation logs once reviewed, or restrict their access to administration personnel only.
- ❑ Modify the XML start-mode attribute in the opmn.xml configuration file to ensure that SSL is enabled for the HTTP Server at startup.
- ❑ Apply the appropriate Windows security template after OAS product components have been successfully installed.
- ❑ Install only Oracle Identity Management when deploying the infrastructure tier into an enterprise environment where the Metadata Repository is already deployed.
- ❑ Install only infrastructure tier product components that are required in order for the system to be mission effective.
- ❑ Assign strong, unique passwords for administration databases created during the installation process.
- ❑ Assign a strong password for the ias_admin administration account.
- ❑ Change the default port assignment for the Oracle Database Listener to obscure this well-known port-to-protocol mapping.
- ❑ Restrict access to the Oracle Database Listener by enabling TCP valid node checking and by specifying IP addresses for servers that have OAS web server, portal and infrastructure tier components installed.
- ❑ As with the infrastructure tier, install only web tier product components that are required in order for the system to be mission effective.
- ❑ Select the configuration option "Only use SSL connections with the Oracle Internet Directory" to protect user account information transferred between OID and the web server tier via LDAP.
- ❑ Once installation is completed, assign strong passwords to all portal administration accounts.

- Once installation is complete, change default passwords assigned to each Database Access Descriptor (DAD), and specify strong passwords as described in Chapter 6 of this security guide.

- Restrict read access to the dads.conf configuration file to administrators only.

- Upon installation of the OAS Portal, verify that the dads.conf configuration file excludes the following packages of PL/SQL stored procedures:

  - PlsqlExclusionList sys.*

  - PlsqlExclusionList dbms_*

  - PlsqlExclusionList utl_*

  - PlsqlExclusionList owa_util.

- Refer to product security updates and vendor configuration guidance for updated information regarding documented PL/SQL vulnerabilities.

- To prevent unauthorized access to cached portal content, configure the portal cache directory to restrict file access to cached pages.

- Select the configuration option "Only use SSL connections with the Oracle Internet Directory" to protect user account information transferred between OID and the OAS Web Cache via LDAP.

## OAS HTTP Server

### Virtual Hosts

- To minimize the use of security configuration overrides by virtual hosts, co-locate virtual hosts containing sensitive content on OAS HTTP Servers configured to protect sensitive content, and virtual hosts containing non-sensitive content on OAS HTTP Servers configured to host non-sensitive content.

- In cases where the virtual host is configured to override the default security settings of the OAS HTTP Server, verify that the virtual host is configured to adequately protect its content based on the sensitivity of that content.

- In cases where the virtual host does not override the default security settings of the OAS HTTP Server, verify that default OAS HTTP Server security settings are sufficient to protect the content provided by that virtual host.

### Apache Software Modules

- Disable Apache software modules that are not required.

- Only install and enable software modules obtained directly from Oracle.

- Do not restrict access to content based on the IP address of the client.

- Enable the mod_osso software module in order for Oracle partner applications to utilize Oracle SSO authentication capabilities.

- Enable the mod_auth software module so that external applications, which cannot utilize SSO authentication functions, can utilize Apache-supported user authentication capabilities.

- Enable the mod_ossl module in order to utilize SSL capabilities

- Enable mod_certheaders if certificate-based, client authentication is performed through the OAS Web Cache.

- ❑ Do not utilize mod_proxy with both forward and reverse proxy functions enabled at the same time. Enable forward proxy capabilities only if restrictions are defined to limit access to internal web servers.
- ❑ Do not use the open source version of mod_security that is bundled with OAS 10g EE in lieu of commercial-grade IDS solutions.

## Directory and File Access

- ❑ Restrict user access to directories where OAS HTTP Server log information is physically stored in order to protect logging data from accidental or malicious modification or deletion.
- ❑ Restrict access to the OAS HTTP Server configuration files httpd.conf and ssl.conf to system administrators only.
- ❑ When changing default directory locations used by the OAS HTTP Server, verify that access permissions for the new directory locations restrict access to administration personnel.

## OAS HTTP Server Configuration Directives

- ❑ Use the Timeout directive to specify a timeout value in the range 60-120 seconds, which is adequate for most deployments.
- ❑ Set ExtendedStatus to Off unless required for performance tuning. If enabled, use the Allow from and Deny from directives described below to restrict access to the HTML output.
- ❑ Use the Port directive to configure standalone HTTP Servers to listen on a port other than the default port.
- ❑ Use the Listen directive to configure the HTTP Listener to utilize a port other than the default port.
- ❑ Use the Directory directive to restrict user access to file system locations containing web content, and to ensure that only authenticated users can view information contained in these directories.
- ❑ Do not use .htaccess files to specify access control information.
- ❑ Specify the client's hostname rather than its IP address when restricting access using the Allow from or Deny from directives.
- ❑ At a minimum, configure the LogFormat directive so that the following information is logged for each HTTP request:
  - ■ The date and time of the request
  - ■ The host name and/or IP address of the client
  - ■ The URL accessed
- ❑ For systems that host sensitive content, configure the LogFormat directive to record additional information required for periodic audit reviews and/or forensic analysis.
- ❑ Periodically review OAS HTTP Server logs in accordance with applicable security policies.
- ❑ For deployments in which OAS Web Cache is running, set UseWebCacheIP to On to ensure that client IP addresses are property logged by the OAS HTTP Server.

### OAS HTTP Server SSL Directives

- ❑ Use the SSLCARevocationFile directive to specify the filename of the Certificate Revocation List (CRL) and assign file permissions that restrict access to administrators only.

- ❑ Use the SSLCARevocationPath directive to specify the file system directory where the CRL file is stored and assign directory permissions that prohibit access to all users.

- ❑ Set the SSLCipherSuite directive to 'ALL:!ADH:!EXPORT56:+HIGH:+MEDIUM-SSLv2' to eliminate use of low-strength ciphers and SSLv2.

- ❑ Set the SSLEngine directive to On if use of SSL is required.

- ❑ Use the SSLLog directive to specify the file where SSL logging information will be stored and assign file permissions that prohibit access by all users.

- ❑ Use the SSLLogLevel directive to set the logging level to collect logging information as needed.

- ❑ Set the SSLMutex directive to sem to enable use of locking semaphores.

- ❑ With the SSLOptions directive, do not enable the FakeBasicAuth option, which allows unauthenticated access to a directory.

- ❑ Set the SSLProtocol directive to ALL –SSLv2 to disable use of SSLv2 protocol.

- ❑ Do not use the SSLRequire directive to conditionally enable use of SSL. Enable use of SSL, using the SSLEngine directive, based on the sensitivity of the data.

- ❑ Enable the SSLRequireSSL directive to force clients to use SSL when accessing a directory.

- ❑ Enable the SSLVerifyClient directive if certificate-based authentication is required.

- ❑ Use the SSLWallet directive to specify the location of the Oracle wallet, and assign directory and file permissions to prohibit access to all users.

## OAS Portal

- ❑ Enable use of SSL throughout the OAS Portal for deployments that handle or process sensitive information.

- ❑ Limit the granting of Manage Content privileges to Oracle users.

- ❑ Enable the Approvals and Notifications page group property for all page groups that potentially incorporate sensitive content.

- ❑ Enable the Override Approval Process page group property only when content published to the page group carries no risk for disclosure of sensitive information, or when content developers are qualified to perform page approvals.

- ❑ If a page approval process is enabled, ensure that the list of approvers includes qualified security review personnel.

- ❑ Enable the Display Page to Public page property only when content published to the page carries no risk for disclosure of sensitive information.

- ❑ Do not enable item level security for a portal page if that page implements functions intended exclusively for a single user, group or functional role.

- ❑ Create functional groups or roles that grant page item read or write access. Assign user membership to these functional groups based on the level of privileges that they require.

- Limit the granting of the manage page item privilege to Oracle users other than the page owner and page item creator.

- Set the expiration period of a page item to be consistent with the volatility of the information it contains. Continued publication expired or out-of-date information diminishes the integrity of the system.

- To restrict access to content through Oracle Ultra Search, assign an ACL to each data source and specifies only those users and groups for which access is granted.

- Assign strong passwords to pre-defined OAS Portal administration accounts. Limit access to Portal administration passwords, and limit user membership in OAS Portal administration groups such as DBA and PORTAL_ADMINISTRATORS.

- If portal user self-registration is enabled, ensure that an approval process is established to evaluate registration requests relative to need-to-know access restrictions that are being enforced.

- Review the set of privileges assigned to each Portal user and administration account to ensure that the right combination of privileges is being granted.

- Limit and periodically review global privileges granted to OAS Portal users.

## OAS Web Cache

- Governing security policies may require user authentication based on client certificates. If so, configure the OAS Web Cache to require client-side certificates.

- Verify that OAS Web Cache and OAS HTTP Server are configured to accept and receive IP address and/or client certificate information from external users, as required.

- If sensitive content is delivered through the OAS Web Cache, enable use of SSL between the OAS Web Cache and external users.

- Consider the tradeoff between throughput performance and the need to protect sensitive content transferred between each origin server and the OAS Web Cache, on a case-by-case basis.

- Enable use of HTTPS when configuring the OAS Web Cache to access an origin server that provides sensitive content, or when governing security policies require end-to-end protection of data as a mitigation strategy for insider threats.

- If the OAS Web Cache is configured to cache both sensitive and non-sensitive content, regard all cached data as sensitive content stored in a high threat environment.

- Configure the OAS Web Cache with caching rules to restrict caching of sensitive information.

- Verify that the use of HTTP Surrogate-Control header directives is consistent with security policies for restricting the caching of sensitive content.

- If caching of dynamic content is required, define expiration rules that establish expiration timeframes consistent with the volatility of the content.

- Verify that the use of HTTP Surrogate-Control header directives in web pages containing dynamic content is consistent with security policies that define enterprise data integrity requirements regarding access to stale dynamic content.

## OAS Identity Management

- ❑ Enable password policy settings to require a user to supply their original password when changing their password.

- ❑ Set the Password Expiry Time to 42 days, which is the standard password expiration period defined in NSA/Windows security templates.

- ❑ Use the Reset Password upon Next Login policy setting to periodically force users to reset account passwords.

- ❑ Enable the Use Reversible Encryption password policy setting only when synchronization between OID and Microsoft Active Directory requires exchange of user password information.

- ❑ Set the Global Lockout Duration and IP Lockout Duration password policy settings to 15 minutes, which is the standard lockout period defined in NSA/Windows security templates.

- ❑ Reduce the Password Maximum Failure and IP Lockout Maximum Failure password policy settings from 10 attempts to 3 attempts.

- ❑ Set the Minimum Number of Characters in Password policy setting to a value between 8 and 12 characters; use longer passwords in deployments where sensitive data is processed.

- ❑ In the absence of capabilities that enforce use of uppercase and/or special characters in passwords, increase the Number of Numeric Characters in Password policy setting from 1 numeric character to 3 numeric characters.

- ❑ Set the Number of Passwords in History policy setting to 24 passwords, which is the standard history length defined in NSA/Windows security templates.

- ❑ Verify that the export connector profile omits from its mapping all sensitive OID user account attributes that are not intended to be exported to Active Directory.

- ❑ Enable secure LDAP to protect user account data being synchronized between OID and Microsoft Active Directory.

- ❑ Verify that valid X.509 certificates are installed in the Microsoft domain controller that is hosting the Active Directory service, which OID is to synchronize with, and in the Oracle Wallet utilized by with Oracle Directory Integration and Provisioning (DIP) service.

- ❑ Enable secure LDAP if password reversible encryption is utilized.

- ❑ Verify that Windows directory permissions restrict access to OID management tools to Windows administration personnel.

- ❑ To configure OID auditing to monitor the system for unauthorized access, enable the following OID audit configuration options:

  - ▪ Superuser login

  - ▪ Bind unsuccessful

  - ▪ Access Violation

- ❑ When directory auditing is enabled, periodically review audit data generated by the Oracle Directory Manager tool.

- ❑ Use the Oracle Directory Manager tool to configure OID to disable anonymous binding.

- ❑ Apply the grantrole.ldif configuration file when configuring OID 10g EE to synchronize user account data with Microsoft Active Directory.

- ❏ . Limit use of the Oracle Directory Manager tool for modifying OID directory ACLs.

- ❏ Verify that SSL is enabled for OAS administration web pages, especially web pages used to configure the SSO Server or Oracle partner applications, or to access OID user account data.

- ❏ Restrict and periodically review user membership in Oracle administration groups, especially global and realm administration groups, which may grant authority over significant numbers of Oracle users.

- ❏ Verify that pre-defined administration roles meet operational requirements of the target deployment. If a new role must be created, make sure that only the minimum set of privileges required for that role is granted to it. Periodically review the assignment of Oracle users to roles that grant administrative privileges.

- ❏ Assign strong passwords to pre-defined Oracle administration accounts. Restrict access to administration password information and take steps to prevent its unauthorized disclosure.

- ❏ if OAS Portal is not installed, disable the PORTAL and PORTAL_ADMIN administration accounts to reduce the risk of unauthorized users gaining administrative access.

# Pre-Defined Privileges, Groups and User Accounts

The following table contains a partial listing of administrative privileges provided with OAS 10g EE. Refer to Oracle product documentation for a complete list of supported privileges and associated functional capabilities.

Table 7.  Administrative Privileges

| Privilege Name | Description |
| --- | --- |
| **Delegated Administration Services (DAS)** | |
| OracleDASCreateUser | Grants ability to create DAS user entries |
| OracleDASEditUser | Grants ability to modify DAS user entries |
| OracleDASDeleteUser | Grants ability to delete DAS user entries |
| OracleDASCreateGroup | Grants ability to create DAS group entries |
| OracleDASEditGroup | Grants ability to modify DAS group entries |
| OracleDASDeleteGroup | Grants ability to delete DAS group entries |
| OracleDASUserPriv | Grants ability to assign access rights to users |
| OracleDASGroupPriv | Grants ability to assign access rights to groups |
| OracleDASConfiguration | Grants ability to configure DAS services user interface |
| OracleManageExtendedPreferences | Grants ability to manage extended preferences |
| **Portal Item Level Privileges** | |
| Manage | Grants the ability to view the item, edit the item, delete the item, and grant privileges on the item. |
| Edit | Grants the ability to view the item, edit the item, and delete the item. |
| View | Grants the ability to view the item. |
| **Portal Page Level Privileges** | |

| Privilege Name | Description |
|---|---|
| Manage Content | Grants the ability to add, edit, hide, show, share, and delete, any item, portlet, or tab on the page. |
| Manage | Grants the Manage Content privilege plus the abilities to control the access and style of the page. |
| Manage Items With Approval | Grants the ability to add or edit items on the page. However, page changes are published only after the approval process is complete. |
| Manage Style | Grants the ability to change the style and region properties on the page. |
| Customize Portlets (Full) | Grants the ability to change the style of a page and to add, delete, move, hide, or show any portlet on the page. |
| Customize Portlets (Add-Only) | Grants the ability to change the style of the page, add portlets to the page, and remove, hide, or show the portlets that are added. |
| Customize Portlets (Hide-Show) | Grants the ability to change the style of the page, and hide, show, or rearrange any portlet on the page. |
| Customization (Style) | Grants the ability to apply a different style to the page. |
| View | Grants the ability to view the content of the page, but not the ability to add, remove, show, or hide any of that content. |
| **Portal Page Group Privileges** | |
| Manage All | Grants all page group privileges: Manage Classifications, Manage Templates, Manage Styles, and View. |
| Manage Classifications | Grants the ability to create, edit, and delete any category, perspective, attribute, custom item type, and custom page type in the page group. A user with this privilege cannot view the pages in this page group unless he or she also has the View privilege. |
| Manage Templates | Grants ability to create, edit, and delete any page template in the page group. This privilege does not assign View access to pages in the page group. |
| Manage Styles | Grants create, edit and delete any style in the page group, and can be used to apply a different style to pages in a page group. Users with this privilege can also view any page in the page group. |
| View | Grants read access to all page in the page |

| Privilege Name | Description |
|---|---|
|  | group, as well as the ability to preview externally published portlet in the page group. A user with this privilege cannot add, remove, show, or hide any content within the pages in the page group. |

## Pre-Defined Administration Groups and Roles

The following table contains a partial listing of pre-defined administration groups and roles provided with OAS 10g EE. Refer to Oracle product documentation for a complete listing of pre-defined administration groups and roles.

**Table 8. Administration Groups Privileges**

| Group Name | Associated Privileges |
|---|---|
| Context Administrators | Grants privileges to administer all entities in this Oracle Context |
| Realm Administrators | Grants realm administrative privileges |
| Super User Administrators | Grants OID super user privileges. |
| User Security Administrators | Grants privileges to administer password-related attributes of users in the Identity Management Realm. |
| DAS Administrators | Granted full DAS privileges |
| DAS Service Administrators | Grants privileges to manage user services. |
| DAS Account Administrators | Grants privileges to enable, disable or unlock Oracle user accounts. |
| Oracle Resource Access Group | Grants self resource management privileges. |
| ASP Administrators | Grants privileges to manage subscribers within a domain. |
| IAS Administrators | Grants IAS administrator privileges |
| DAS Privilege Group | Grants full DAS privileges, including privileges to grant DAS privileges to other users. |
| Authenticated Users | Grants default privileges that are assigned to all authenticated Oracle users. |
| DBA | Grants privileges to create, edit, delete and modify user and group privileges, and privileges to configure distributed access services. The DBA group is part of the Portal Administrators group. |
| Instant Portal Administrators | Grants privileges to administer Oracle Instant Portals and create and manage users in any Oracle Instant Portal.. |
| Collaboration Suite Users | Assigns the Oracle Collaboration Suite home page as the Oracle user's default page. |
| Reports Administrators | Grants privileges to manage report services. These services include reports, printers, calendars, and servers. |

| | |
|---|---|
| Reports Users | Grants privileges to use OAS report services. |
| Reports Developers | Grants privileges to develop reports. |
| Reports Power Users | Grants privileges to modify report service reports. |
| UDDI Administrators | Grants administrative privileges to the UDDI Registry. |
| UDDI Publishers | Grants privileges required to invoke the publishing API of the UDDI Registry. |
| UDDI Replicators | Grants privileges to configure UDDI replication capabilities. . |
| UDDI Unlimited Quota Users Group | Grants privileges to publish entries to the UDDI Registry. |
| Portal Administrators | Grants global OAS Portal privileges and a subset of OAS administrative privileges, excluding SSO administrative privileges. |
| Portlet Publishers | Grants OAS Portal privileges required to publish portlets. |
| Portal Developers | Grants OAS Portal privileges required to create portal providers and manage shared components. |

## Pre-defined User and Administration Accounts

The following table contains a partial listing of pre-defined user and administration accounts provided with OAS 10g EE. Refer to Oracle product documentation for a complete listing.

**Table 9.  Predefined User and Administration Accounts**

| Account | Purpose |
|---|---|
| PUBLIC | User account associated with unauthenticated users of the OAS Portal. Once authenticated, the user name changes from PUBLIC to the authenticated user name. |
| PORTAL | This is the Portal super user account. This account is granted all the global privileges available in the OAS Portal. This user is also an Oracle Instant Portal administrator for every Oracle Instant Portal, regardless of who created them. |
| PORTAL_ADMIN | This is a Portal administration account intended for users who manage pages and provision Portal user accounts. This account is granted Portal privileges, excluding those that provide the ability to obtain higher privileges or perform database operations. A PORTAL_ADMIN cannot edit any page groups or manage schemas or shared objects. |
| DIPADMIN | Administration account associated with Oracle Directory and Integration (DIP) service. DIPADMIN is a member of the Directory Integration and Provisioning Administrator group |

| | |
|---|---|
| CN=ORCLADMIN | The OID super user account assigns all privileges required to manage the OID. This administration account is a member of the repository owners group, DAS Components Owners Group, and iASAdmins Group. This account has access to the Oracle Directory Manager tool. |
| ORCLADMIN | This account is distinct from "CN=ORCLADMIN" and grants global privileges in OAS Portal. This account is created for the Oracle Application Server administrators, and uses the password that is supplied during the Oracle Application Server installation. This user is also an Instant Portal administrator for every Oracle Instant Portal, regardless of who created them. |
| IAS_Admin | This account has administrative privileges and is used to manage OAS core services. |

# List of Acronyms

ACL – Access Control List
AES - Advanced Encryption Standard
AJP – Apache JServ Protocol
API – Application Program Interface
CA – Certificate Authority
CIS – Center for Internet Security
CRL – Certificate Revocation File
CNSS - Committee on National Security Systems
DAD – Database Access Descriptor
DAS – Delegated Administration Service
DHCP – Dynamic Host Configuration Protocol
DN – Distinguished Name
DoD - Department of Defense
DISA - Defense Information Systems Agency
DMZ – De-Militarized Zone
FIPS – Federal Information Processing Standards
FTP – File Transfer Protocol
HTML – Hypertext Markup Language
HTTP – Hypertext Transfer Protocol
IDS – Intrusion Detection System
JDBC – Java Database Connectivity
J2EE – Java 2, Enterprise Edition
LDAP – Lightweight Directory Access Protocol
NIST - National Institute of Standards and Technology
NSA – National Security Agency
OAS - Oracle Application Server
OCA – Oracle Certificate Authority
OC4J – Oracle Containers for J2EE
OID – Oracle Internet Directory
PKI – Public Key Infrastructure
PL/SQL – Procedural Language/Structured Query Language
RBAC – Role Based Access Control
SNAC – System and Network Attack Center
SSL - Secure Socket Layer
SSO – Single Sign-On
TCP – Transmission Control Protocol
XML – Extensible Markup Language

# References

June 2003, *National Policy on the Use of Advanced Encryption Standard (AES) to Protect National Security Systems and National Security Information*, Policy No. 15, Fact Sheet No. 1, CNSS.

December 2002, *Security Requirements for Cryptographic Modules*, FIPS Pub 140-2, National Institute of Standards and Technology (NIST).

June 2005, *Guidelines for the Selection and Use of Transport Layer Security (TLS) Implementations*, Special Publication 800-52, National Institute of Standards and Technology (NIST).

March 2003, *Recommended Standard Application Security Requirements*, Draft Version 2.0, Defense Information Systems Agency (DISA).

January 2006, *Application Services Security Technical Implementation Guide (STIG)*, Version 1, Release 1, Defense Informaton Systems Agency (DISA).

August 2005, *Application Services Security Checklist*, Version 2, Release 1.7, Defense Information Systems Agency (DISA).

April 2005, *WEB Server Checklist and Procedures*, Version 5.0, Release 1, Defense Information Systems Agency (DISA).

March 2006, *Active Directory Security Technical Implementation Guide*, Version 1 Release 1, DISA.

Ivan Ristic, March 2005, *Apache Security*, O'Reilly Media, Inc.

Center for Internet Security, *Benchmark for Oracle 9i/10g*, Version 2

Saad Syed, Peter Goatly, May 2006, *Security Target for Oracle Application Server 10g (9.0.4)*, Issue 1.0, Oracle Corporation.

Stock, A., July 2005, *A Guide to Building Secure Web Applications and Web Services*, 2.0, The Open Web Application Security Project (OWASP).

Perry, E.H., December 2004, *Oracle Application Server Security Guide, 10g R2*, B13999-01, Oracle Corporation.

Van Raalte, T., November 2004, *Oracle Application Server Performance Guide, 10g R2*, B14001-01, Oracle Corporation.

Van Raalte, T., Ward, R., Deval, R., et.al., December 2004, *Oracle Application Server 10g High Availability Guide*, B14003-01, Oracle Corporation.

Roberson, T., November 2004, *Oracle Application Server Concepts 10g R2*, B13994-01, Oracle Corporation.

Schaefer, H., May 2005, *Oracle HTTP Server Administrator's Guide 10g R2*, B14007-02, Oracle Corporation.

Grembowicz, H., Laquerre, P., Pond, J., et. al, May 2005, *Oracle Application Server Administrator's Guide 10g R2*, B13995-02, Oracle Corporation.

Steiner, D., December 2004, *Oracle Application Server Web Cache Administrator's Guide 10g R2*, B14046-01, Oracle Corporation.

Desmond, E., Smith, R., December 2004, *Oracle Internet Directory Administrator's Guide 10g R2*, B14082-01, Oracle Corporation.

Abrecht, H., December 2004, *Oracle Application Server Single Sign-On Administrator's Guide 10g R2*, B14078-01, Oracle Corporation.

Lubbers, P., December 2004, *Oracle Application Server Portal Configuration Guide 10g R2*, B14037-01, Oracle Corporation.

Desmond, E., Strohm, R., December 2004, *Oracle Identity Management Concepts and Deployment Planning Guide 10g R2*, B14084-01, Oracle Corporation.

Smith, R., December 2004, *Oracle Identity Management Guide to Delegated Administration 10g R2*, B14086-01, Oracle Corporation.

Gosselin, D., December 2004, *Oracle Identity Management Integration Guide 10g R2*, B14085-01, Oracle Corporation.